Please Hold:
The Power of Outcome-Driven Thinking

By Fabrício Laguna

Published by International Institute of Business Analysis, Pickering, Ontario, Canada.

© 2025 Fabricio Laguna. All rights reserved.

Print Edition: ISBN-978-1-927584-40-8
eBook Edition: ISBN-978-1-927584-41-5

To my beloved wife, Tetê, the most outcome-driven person I know. What I strive to achieve with techniques and rational thought comes effortlessly to her.

Contents

Prologue

While life might seem to happen by chance, I have observed that most events are, in fact, the result of our conscious decisions. I'm still amazed by the professional success I have achieved, going from a simple call center agent to transformation manager in one of the largest organizations in the country in just a few months.

People might attribute my rapid ascent to luck. In other words, chance favored me, and others could not replicate my success. I don't deny that I have been lucky. I have met phenomenal professionals who have put their faith in me, and I have been inspired by charismatic mentors who set the bar high in their example. Moreover, I was in a place and time ripe for transformation and got to play a pivotal role.

However, it would be unfair to attribute my success purely to luck. Allow me to disagree with this line of thinking and present my arguments in this book. A person who experienced the same situations I did but had a different way of seeing the world might classify as misfortunes the opportunities I embraced. My success was not the result of fortune but a way of thinking, feeling, and acting I have developed that can be replicated by anyone who wants to achieve similar success, independent of the context.

By the end of this book, you can decide for yourself. If you see it too, I hope my story inspires your personal development and the growth of a more responsible and sustainable culture.

An Outcome-Driven Mindset can jumpstart a career, but far more importantly, it can transform the world, creating better results for everyone.

Chapter 1: Routine

Summer had barely begun, but I knew my shirt would be soaked in sweat as soon as it touched my back.

"Why can't we wear something cooler to work?" I thought, as I got ready for another day.

Instantly in my head, as normal as can be, I saw everyone at the Call Center in their swimwear, being lightly refreshed by the sprinkler system as we attended customer calls. My amusement at the assorted swimming attire was rudely interrupted by the appearance of my boss, Mr. Andrade. Wearing a thick life jacket and blowing furiously on a whistle, he sprinted over to my cubicle to administer an official reprimand. Startled, I deleted the uninvited vision from my mind.

"At least the office has air con! Geez, I could do with one here. This heat is killing me." I immediately relegated the idea of having air conditioning at home to the impossible dream shelf, together with all the other comforts and experiences I would love to have but would never be part of the life of an ordinary person like me.

Before leaving, I grabbed a coffee with milk and some bread and butter. The butter, straight out of the fridge, was like a rock. Unable to spread it, I pared off some shavings and positioned them strategically over the bread. Of course, leaving the butter out of the fridge would have been better, but I didn't have the nerve. I'd rather face a block of ice than a rancid soup of bacteria. The butter went back into the fridge.

On the way out, I passed the gorgeous girl from the sixth floor. She had been at the desk in the lobby, asking about a delivery. That day, she was in a turquoise dress that accentuated the color of her eyes. I noticed her flip-flops and knew she hadn't been out. She had just come down to talk to the doorman. She wasn't wearing make-up and, in my eyes, didn't need any. "Divine works don't need retouching," I thought.

She passed right by me with a light good morning and a friendly smile. I fumbled for words, trying to make an everyday thing of stepping out of the elevator and freezing, awestruck, gazing at her. God, what would she think of me? Psycho? Stalker? Creep? But then, I didn't want to come off as cold and standoffish either. I needed to say something relaxed and natural. She'd find me warm, approachable, and self-assured. A good-humored comment would be perfect! I mean, everyone wants to be around amusing, easy-going people, right? Now, what fun remark would go down best?

Me: Good m—

And that was it. The elevator door cut off the budding exchange.

"One more for the impossible dream shelf," I thought, and resignedly set off for the subway. "She's way out of my league anyway."

At the subway station, half a dozen people were already lined up at the ticket desk. Luckily, the ticket machines were practically empty, so I joined the line. Two of the five machines were working, and there were just two people in front of me.

"This'll be quick," I thought. One of the people was an old lady, and the other looked like a tourist. While I was waiting, I reflected that there ought to be signs stating the prerequisites for joining the ticket-machine line:

> **Do not enter this line if:**
> 1. You do not understand the local language.
> 2. You do not use digital devices.
> 3. You do not know anything about this subway system.
> 4. You do not have time-sensitive components in your day.
> 5. You do not want to piss me off.

As the minutes passed, the old lady and the tourist dropped at hurdle after hurdle, and, of course, the line at the ticket desk was moving along nicely. I stood there watching passengers leaving, tickets in their hands, while I contemplated my life choices. Eventually, a subway employee appeared to help, and the pair managed to conclude their purchases and liberate the ticket machines. Using my debit card, I resolutely bought ten tickets and at least a week's salvation from a repeat performance. I didn't buy more because my funds were low, and I didn't want to run out of cash. It was better to wait until payday before spending any more.

On the train, people were squeezing and shoving themselves through the doors, trying to find a sliver of space in the suffocating metal canister. I watched in anguish as a girl fought against the inflowing tide of passengers, not managing to get off the train. It was chaos. A tall young man noticed her plight and leaned aside, allowing her to escape just seconds before the doors closed. A heavy crowd was still left outside waiting for the next train. "Damn rush hour," I thought, as the train swayed and I steadied myself, buffeted by the bodies pressed around me.

I jumped out at Central Station, already short on time if I didn't want to be late for work. Luckily, the bank's Call Center was only a few blocks away.

In the street, I saw the old lady who was always there asking for spare change in front of the post office. Well, she didn't ask exactly. She offered us the opportunity to leave contributions in a small box at her feet in exchange for sharing her musical artistry. She played a four-stringed toy guitar that was totally out of tune and sang, in her peculiar way, the same song every day, just the chorus:

> *Let life take me; life takes me.*
> *Let life take me; life takes me.*
> *Let life take me; life takes me...*
> *Happy and grateful for all that God gave me.[1]*

---

1. "Deixa a Vida Me Levar" (Let Life Take Me), a song by Zeca Pagodinho.

I could never get a handle on that lady. Did she think her music was street art appreciated by the passersby? Had she considered learning to play an instrument properly? Or was the idea that we pay her to stop the noise? And the strangest thing, the thing that I always wondered, was: What did she have to be so grateful for if she lived on the streets and had absolutely nothing?

It was a fleeting moment—just a hundred yards from where I went into the bank, swiped my card at the turnstile, clocked in, and headed up to the third floor, where the Call Center was.

Mr. Andrade was already off on his morning rounds to check that everyone was at their desk, carrying out their tasks according to departmental guidelines. If the Call Center goals were met, he would get a bonus at the end of the year. Although it wasn't much, it was enough for him to hassle us every day and make a misery of our daily existence.

Our performance indicators included things like:

- Occupancy Rate
- Total Number of Calls Answered
- Average Handling Time (AHT)
- Average Waiting Time (AWT)

The shorter the AHT, the better. That way, more calls can be answered by fewer agents. If there are a lot of calls in the queue waiting for an available agent and the AHT is too long, the AWT tends to grow.

Our team was sorely understaffed for the volume of calls we handled. Even with an occupancy rate nearing 100%, the

AWT was well above the goal, but Mr. Andrade had developed a strategy to address this problem. We were instructed to end any call that hadn't been concluded after about five minutes and answer another one. We had to hang up and record that the phone system had cut off the call. The customer would then have to call back to solve their problem, increasing the number of calls answered and simultaneously reducing the AHT and AWT. Goals met and bonus guaranteed. Genius! Provided you didn't have to deal with the customer personally, which is what I did all day long.

> Me: State Bank, good morning. May I have your branch and account number, please?
>
> Customer: Do I really have to repeat that? I've just given that information to your robot.
>
> Me: I'm sorry, ma'am. It's a security measure.

I lied. The robot she was referring to is an IVR (Interactive Voice Response)—a system that handles incoming calls automatically. This system isn't integrated with our human service system, so none of the information provided by the customer at the first stage is transferred. We have to ask for it all over again. Sound ridiculous? Welcome to my life!

> Me: How can I assist you today, Ms. Souza?
>
> Customer: I can't believe I have to explain this again! This is the fifth time I've called you about the same problem, and the call always gets cut off before you sort anything out. It's disgraceful!
>
> Me: I'm really sorry about that, Ms. Souza. The telephone

system has been a little unstable over the past few days.

I lied once more and blamed the telephone company. How low can you get? I checked the customer's call history and saw she was lying, too. It wasn't the fifth time she had called, only the third. She was trying to pressure me. Nevertheless, I'm sure three times was more than enough to annoy the hell out of her.

Customer: It's been months since I informed you of my change of address, but my credit card bills are still being delivered to my old address.

Me: I see that you have already requested to change the address of your checking account. Would you also like to change the address of your credit card bill?

Customer: Of course I would! I'm the one who moved, not my checking account, my credit card, or my car insurance. I moved, and all my mail should come to my new address.

Me: I understand, Ms. Souza. Could you please hold the line for just a moment?

Cursed systems and their non-integrated databases! How wonderfully straightforward it would be if you changed the customer's address in one place and it was applied across the board, but that's not how it works. Behind the façade, checking accounts, credit cards, and insurance are all operated by different teams with independent systems and just-about-tolerable integration. To the customer, it all looks like the State Bank, the brand they bought into, but these companies have been brought in over decades in a wholly disorganized manner. The result is a patchwork of processes, systems, and databases that is barely workable.

I rang an agent from the Credit Card Service Center.

> Me: Hi, I'm here with a customer who needs her card address changed to match her checking account address.

> C.C. Agent: Access the credit card services system and open a request under "Customer Data Change." In the body of the request, include the card number and the new address.

This card team won't do anything unless we log a request into the system. I bet if their office block caught fire, you'd have to log a request for them to sound the fire alarm.

> Me: Is that all?

> C.C. Agent: Yeah. The address will be updated within two working days.

> Me: Oh. It isn't immediate, then?

> C.C. Agent: Our SLA[2] for customer data changes is two working days. If it's urgent, attach an urgent request form signed by a director, and I'll see what we can do.

> Me: No, that's fine. We'll stick with the standard wait time, thank you.

God forbid I should fill out another form and attempt to get one of the directors' signatures. It would take way longer than two days. Directors are mythical beings like fairies and unicorns.

---

2. SLA: A service level agreement is a commitment made by a service provider.

They're never seen in the corridors and there's some debate surrounding their true powers. I might as well send a letter to Santa Claus and hang on until Christmas for the change of address. Better to wait for the standard time of the service level agreement, but I would need to get some additional information from the customer to open the request.

> Me: Thank you for holding, Ms. Souza. Could I please take your credit card details?

> Customer: Don't you have the number there?

> Me: As I said before, it's a security measure.

It's amazing how once you've been lying shamelessly for a while, it seems to stop weighing on your conscience, perhaps because the truth would be far more shocking for the customer.

Thinking that I'm protecting her security will make her much happier than knowing I don't have access to a single byte of the data I need to process her request. "My God, what have I become?!"

With the credit card number jotted down on a notepad, I searched the intranet for the Credit Card Service Request System, at which point I discovered there were three available systems with that name in our company. "Damn it!" Navigating the bank's systems was like wearing hiking boots to a dinner dance—awkward and ill-fitting.

The first system was apparently for corporate cards. The second was some type of benefit card for bank employees. "I didn't know we had that! I need to find out if I'm eligible for any benefits I'm not getting. Just a quick look to see if there's anything useful... I'll bookmark this address and come back later to find out more." The third system was probably what the credit card agent had referred to. It had better be, because time was passing and the customer was waiting.

I entered the system, opened a new request titled "Customer Data Change," copied the credit card number from my notepad, and pasted it into the body of the email. I accessed the Customer Service System, verified Ms. Souza's data, and tried to select the registered address, but the address field was locked and wouldn't allow me to copy and paste the text. "Geez, what crappy software!" The only option was to type the address manually, switching back and forth between windows: "Oscar Neymar... Nieimaier... Niemeyer... Crumbs, what a difficult street name! I hope I haven't misspelled it. Request registered for change of address. Right, that leaves the change of car insurance address."

> Me: Thank you for holding, Ms. Souza. Could you please provide me with the license plate of your insured car?

This time, she didn't even argue. Customers are like that. They start out mad, but as the waiting drags on, they become more docile, afraid of getting cut off again. Sometimes, I notice their energy being consumed like a flashlight about to go out, and I feel sorry for them. It's as if we're sinking in the same boat.

I called the insurance agent, but my heart started racing when I saw Mr. Andrade approaching my cubicle. My handling time was already way over his five-minute goal, and if he told me to hang up, the customer would have to call yet again to sort out the insurance address.

Insurance agent: Insurance services, good afternoon.

Me: Good afternoon. I need to change the address on a customer's car insurance policy.

Insurance agent: What type of insurance is it?

Me: Automobile.

Insurance agent: No sweat. Give me the license plate number and the new address, and I'll change it for you.

Me: Really? Right now?

Insurance agent: Yep, no problem. For home insurance, I'd have to transfer you to another department, but with car insurance, I can change it here.

As I spelled out that difficult street name, I felt a small sense of victory that the addresses would finally be updated. As if it were my own personal triumph against the challenges of life. Something productive would have come out of my day after all. At least one thing in this interaction would be sorted out straight away. My effort had not been in vain. I imagined Ms. Souza smiling radiantly and making a heart sign to me with both hands while everyone in the office applauded the success of my mission. I was showered with confetti and streamers as Mr. Andrade served me a glass of champagne.

Mr. Andrade: This call needs to end, or you'll wreck the AHT.

Me: Yes, Mr. Andrade. I'm just wrapping up.

Back in reality, Mr. Andrade was positioned in front of me, tapping his index finger on his watch and making throat-cutting gestures. I hurried to conclude the call and share the good news with Ms. Souza.

> Me: Thank you for your patience, Ms. Souza. I'm pleased to inform you that your address has been updated on your car insurance policy and, within two working days, will also be updated on your credit card to 418 Oscar Niemeyer Avenue, Apt 1040, where all your correspondence will now be directed.

Customer: Oscar Niemeyer Avenue? That's not my current address. That one's even older. I haven't lived there since before my daughter was born.

Chapter 2: Coffee and Indignation

Call center workers are required by law to take a break from time to time. That day, during our break, HR's convivial matriarch Clarice showed up and gave us each a chocolate bar. Once a week the bank would try to sweeten us up a little. I put my candy bar away in my bag for later. During this time, I usually have coffee with my friend Rodrigo, who works in the cubicle next to mine.

There's a coffee machine at the end of the hallway, where you can press a button and get an espresso. Okay, I wouldn't say it was great coffee. In fact, there might be coffee connoisseurs who would argue that it isn't coffee at all—more like hot, dirty, over-sweetened water. But at least it gives us some energy to carry on with our work. While my colleague patiently pressed the button and waited for the coffee machine, I was already heated up and ready to let off steam.

> Me: I can't take this anymore, Rodrigo. I feel like I'm on an exercise bike—I'm pedaling like hell, but I don't go anywhere. It's a never-ending cycle. I spend every day

talking to pissed-off people and leaving them even more pissed off. Give me some hope here, man. How was your day?

Rodrigo: Today? Um... Well, today was pretty cool. This morning, I had mushrooms and chives in my scrambled eggs. Man, it was awesome!

Perhaps I should mention that Rodrigo's lifelong passion is cooking. For him, food is inspiring. If you want to share recipes and organize dinners, he's your guy. I'm often in awe of his fascination with different ingredients and flavors. But that was not the topic I had in mind. I was searching for inspiration, for some higher meaning to lift us, right there, above this empty toiling for a measly salary.

Me: That's nice, Rodrigo. But I mean... professionally.

Rodrigo: Oh, right! Professionally. Alrighty. Well, that was productive, too. Today, I changed my photo on LinkedIn. You know that front view where I looked like such a dude? So, now I'm kind of in semi-profile with this smoldering vibe. Here, check it out on my phone. People are even commenting.

Me: The person who commented is your mom.

Rodrigo: The most important person in the world.

The photos were both distinctly off-putting. The front view looked like a startled animal caught in headlights. In the side view, a shadow covered half of his inexplicable and somewhat disturbing expression. However, to avoid losing focus, I temporarily ignored the very long conversation that was my duty as a friend. Instead, I took my cup of hot, dirty water and stirred it slowly.

> Me: I'm talking about what you've done professionally here. At the company.

> Rodrigo: Yeah, me too. I swapped out my LinkedIn photo here. I had nothing to do while I was waiting for the mortgage agent to get back to me. These wait times are the most productive moments of my day. I update LinkedIn and check out my Insta and Face.

I must tell you something you might not be aware of: bank customers get incredibly annoyed when holding the line for extended periods, waiting to sort out their problems during service calls. Little do they know about our life as first-level responders. We have little autonomy to resolve things ourselves and have to activate other agents from specific areas. Unfortunately, these second-level agents are even more tied up, so our calls are queued as we wait to speak to them. In other words, our life consists of stretches of waiting, with an irate customer on the line, for a problem to be solved, and in between, drinking bad coffee.

> Me: Rodrigo, I don't think you're getting it. I want to know about customer service. You know, the calls you got from customers who asked for your help with their problems. That's our profession. That's what we do. Tell me how you helped someone solve a real problem today.

> Rodrigo: Ah! Well, there was a lady who wanted to access Internet Banking, but her password had expired.

Me: Yeah, that's what I'm talking about. How did you help her?

Rodrigo: I said she would need to go to the branch in person to register a new password.

Me: So, you didn't actually solve her problem. You just created another one. Now, in addition to not being able to access IB, she has to go to the branch, which is precisely what she wanted to avoid by using the Internet.

Rodrigo: Well... I guess if you put it like that... it wasn't exactly a solution. Let me think of another one... There was a guy who wanted to find out about a mortgage for an apartment.

Me: Now that's more like it. What did you do?

Rodrigo: I told him to go to his local branch to talk to an account manager.

Me: God help us! You sent him to his local branch, too? Why didn't you just tell him the fees?

Rodrigo: Because the guidelines state we should forward it to an account manager, who will pre-register the customer, assess the credit risk, and calculate the personalized rates. It's not a matter for Call Center service. It's customer relations.

Me: So what is our job?

I don't know if Rodrigo got what I was referring to because he didn't answer. He gave me a slightly hunted look, as if he had no idea what I wanted, and then stared hard at the ceiling, trying to find it anyway. I could feel him searching his memory for a more encouraging scenario to cheer me up. The point of my questions was the fulfillment of a purpose. It was about generating value for customers and the company. That was it. I wanted to feel that our work generated some value.

Rodrigo: There was this old guy who wanted to know his account balance.

Me: But balance is an automatic service carried out in the IVR [that robot I mentioned in the previous chapter]. We don't even have access to that—God knows why not—probably for security reasons. Why did you even attend to him?

Rodrigo: Well. He said that he'd already checked the balance in the IVR, but the amount wasn't what he'd expected.

Me: And what did you do?

Rodrigo: I told him to go find his account manager at the local branch.

God in heaven, what an unworthy lot is ours! Rodrigo's cases were no different from mine. Destined to spend our days supposedly solving problems but, in reality, solving nothing at all. Sending the customer to solve the problem at their local branch. How absolutely perfect for a remote service. Perhaps the miserable salary they pay me—not enough for me to buy an air conditioner for my apartment—is, in fact, an exorbitant salary when compared to the value I generate for the company and the service I offer to customers. Maybe I should have made a formal complaint about my salary to Mr. Andrade, demanding that he pay me *less*.

> Me: It's perplexing to think that no one here actually solves any problems.

> Rodrigo: We don't get paid to solve problems. We get paid to answer the phone and follow the script. Period. What we have to do is meet the Call Center goals and keep Mr. Andrade happy with his Christmas bonus so he doesn't get on our case. I'm good with that!

> Me: Well, I'm not. The whole thing is so frustrating!

"I don't want to feel ashamed of what I do," I thought. "Of course, I should be paid for the value I offer to the company and the customers, but for that to happen, my effort must generate some value, and I'm not at all sure that it does."

My outrage toward my work was becoming unbearable. I could no longer respect myself if nothing I did had the slightest value—poorly integrated systems, bureaucratic processes, and indicators that measured nothing of importance. I was just another cog in a machine that minced up illusions and spat out frustration. What on Earth was I doing there? Why do things have to be this way? Couldn't they somehow be different?

At the height of my rebellion came a flicker of hope, and I decided to turn my indignation into action. Crumpling the plastic coffee cup, I cast it in the recyclable bin, stood up purposefully, and pointed the index finger of my right hand in Rodrigo's direction, pausing dramatically so my weighty words would be forever engraved on his memory.

Me: I have made a decision, and I'm swearing to it here and now. Are you listening? We're going back to our workstations, and I'm solving the problem of the first customer I serve. I don't care what it is; I'm sorting it out—without sending them to the local branch, without hanging up, without lying. I will do whatever it takes to resolve their problem during the call, and I will be honest with them.

Rodrigo's eyes bulged, and his clenched lips contorted downward as a hilarious succession of emotions played over his face: surprise at how indignant I could be regarding what, to him, was just our normal daily life; admiration for my ceremonious pledge to do what boiled down to the basics of our job; and disbelief because, after so many years in that exact job, he was completely resigned to the fact that no real customer problems were going to be solved. Period.

Rodrigo: Alrighty. Good luck with that!

We went back to our cubicles and logged back into our workstations. I gave Rodrigo one last look before enabling the system to receive calls and clenched my right fist in a gesture of commitment to the challenge. He gave an indecipherable smile and began to answer a call.

I enabled the system and prayed that the first customer would have a problem that was easy to solve. That's not exactly what happened.

Chapter 3: The Call That Changed Everything

The system directs calls to agents randomly, so the man who happened to be next in line was sent to me.

Me: State Bank, good morning. Can you tell me your branch and account number, please?

Customer: Sure.

When I typed the data into the system, I saw that the account belonged to a certain Maria Costa Lima. It clearly wasn't the person on the other end of the line.

Me: Can you please confirm the full name of the account holder?

Customer: Yes. Her name is Maria Costa Lima. It's my mother's account. She can't speak right now, so I'm helping her.

Me: Okay. Could you tell me your name, please?

Customer: Oscar.

Me: How can I help you, Oscar?

Somewhat shaken and short of breath, he told me that his mother had just been hospitalized with a suspected stroke and that she was unconscious. Although an elderly lady, she had always been quite independent and managed her financial life without assistance. However, that morning, she had called her son, very distressed, saying that she had been getting messages from the bank about transactions she didn't recognize. Elderly people are the preferred target of scammers and Mrs. Maria Lima had heard countless stories from friends who had fallen victim. She was so distressed that her son had thought it best to stop by her apartment to calm her down and help find out what was happening.

Upon arriving at the apartment, Oscar had found his mother unconscious and immediately called an ambulance. He knew she had health insurance with the bank, but he didn't have the policy number. He could only find the checking account card in her purse and had called our Call Center for help.

Oscar: I need her health insurance card or policy number for the hospital. I don't even know if her insurance covers this kind of care. Can you help me?

It wasn't even a question of being able to help. I had to. I had made a commitment, and here was an urgent issue to be resolved—something that would make me contribute something of value to someone who truly needed it.

Me: Of course. I'll help you with whatever you need.

I empathized with the client. "What if it was my mother?" I thought. But I also needed to make sure I wasn't the one getting hustled. A situation like this requires an identity check to ensure I was indeed talking to the client's son and not a fraudster. In addition, I would have to deal with the absence of formal authorization. The bank would require a series of documents for Oscar to access his mother's data.

I asked the standard security questions associated with the account, such as the account holder's date of birth, address, and phone number. Oscar knew the answers, and that would be enough to provide him with at least some limited general information about the account without revealing sensitive details until he had formal authorization.

> Me: Please give me one minute to find out the policy number and the level of coverage offered by your mother's insurance.

> Oscar: Thank you. I'll be waiting on the line.

I called the insurance agent and was lucky to get the same person I had spoken to in the morning to change Ms. Souza's address. "This guy is good!" I thought. "He'll give me that information in no time."

> Insurance Agent: Sorry, but health insurance isn't in the same system as auto insurance. I don't have access to that information here. Accessing a health insurance policy based on branch and account numbers is only possible at a branch.

Branch, branch, branch... That last word echoed like a death knell to solving my client's problem. "I refuse to refer Oscar to a branch," I thought. He already had enough to deal with, admitting his mother to the hospital under such distressing conditions. It would be unacceptable.

I jotted down some information on a sheet of paper, locked my computer screen, and got up to leave my cubicle.

Rodrigo: Where are you going?

Me: I'm just going to the ground floor branch, and then I'll be right back.

Rodrigo: What... now? During office hours? You can only go out on your break time.

I looked around to see if I could sneak out unnoticed.

Me: If Mr. Andrade asks about me, tell him I've got the runs and went to the restroom.

I took the stairs for fear of running into someone in the elevator and having to explain why I was deserting my post in the middle of the day. The bank has a branch on the ground floor dedicated mainly to servicing employee accounts. The account manager had played soccer with me a few times, and we'd developed a degree of friendship beyond the strictly professional. I could ask for a personal favor. As long as it wasn't anything illegal, he wouldn't deny me help.

Account Manager: Hey, man! Long time no see! How come you're not at the game on Thursdays anymore?

Me: Yeah. I haven't been able to make it, Cesar. I injured my knee and fell out of shape. You know how it is. I miss the exercise, though—need to get back to it. Anyway, I wanted to talk to you about something else. I need your help—not as an athlete but as an account manager.

Account Manager: Sure thing. Are you going to get a loan for that air conditioner you're always talking about? We have a special interest rate for employees that's worth a look.

"What a great idea!" I thought, enjoying the cold, even temperature of the branch and thinking about the sauna waiting for me at home. But that wasn't the reason I was there. The client's son was on hold at my workstation a few floors up, having his mother admitted to the hospital and being questioned for her insurance details.

I quickly explained the situation to Cesar, who empathized with the story and was astonished that we didn't have access to this data in our service system and that not even the insurance agent could pass it on to me.

Me: Yeah, you'd be shocked at how much essential information we don't have access to and how difficult it is to get that data to provide a service!

Account Manager: Here. I've jotted down the health insurance policy number, the card number, and the name of the plan taken out by Mrs. Maria Costa Lima. This information will help her son identify what the insurance covers and finalize the hospital admission.

Me: Wonderful! I'll run back upstairs and pass this information on to him.

Account Manager: Go for it. But tell him if he wants to check those suspicious transactions that caused his mother's collapse, he'll need formal authorization to access the account. Otherwise, no dice.

Me: Like power of attorney?

Account Manager: Something like that. With power of attorney, he can access the Internet Banking of his mother's account and consult everything directly on his phone. But since she's unconscious, he won't get her signature on the power of attorney. It's a bit more complicated. You know who can help you with this? Oswald, from the Legal Department on the eighth floor. Ask him to explain it.

God, I hate the legal people—unbearably bureaucratic with the sole mission of avoiding risk. When in doubt, the answer is always "no can do." There is always a legal restriction, a missing document, or a paragraph of an article of a given normative precedent that requires something else so that you'll never be able to do anything. But that day, I had made a commitment, and I intended to keep it. I would talk to whoever I needed to!

The three flights of stairs were much more tiring on the way up than on the way down. I returned to my workstation out of breath. While logging into my computer, Rodrigo informed me that Mr. Andrade had asked for me during my absence and that the attack of the runs excuse had been implemented. I had better be careful. Mr. Andrade would be on my back.

I resumed the call.

Me: Hello, Oscar. I'm so sorry to keep you waiting. I've managed to get your mother's health insurance details.

Oscar: It was quite a wait! I thought you'd forgotten about me. What took so long?

This question would require a little lie to avoid exposing the fragility of the bank's service structure and tarnishing its reputation. But I had promised that I would solve customers' problems without lying. I briefly told him about the difficulty of accessing information in the first- and second-level service and my secret mission to the branch, where I appealed to the manager's soccer friendship to get the information he needed.

Oscar: Seriously? I didn't know it was as complicated as that. Thank you for the effort.

Oscar said these words in such a slow and reflective way that I felt that, at that moment, it was he who was feeling sorry for me, as if he was imagining my effort to help him. I felt somehow rewarded by his thanks. And I felt a kind of connection that I had never had with a customer before. Somehow, we formed a sort of team dedicated to solving the problems of Mrs. Maria Lima, who, at that moment, could not take care of herself. We were her guardians and would not rest until she was safe.

Me: The health insurance policy is first-rate, and the hospital care will undoubtedly be covered. Just present the policy number to the hospital, and they will handle everything. Now, let's talk about those suspicious transactions that scared your mother and put her in this situation.

Oscar: I have no idea what they were about. She didn't give me details when we spoke on the phone. I tried to access her phone to see if I could see the messages, but it's locked, and I don't know the password.

Me: Are you also a State Bank customer?

Oscar: Yes. I have a strong relationship with the bank.

I found his use of the term "strong relationship" curious, to say the least. Was he an established customer who had acquired multiple products? Or someone who really likes the brand? It was better to leave those thoughts aside and focus on the objective answer: *Yes.*

Me: As a customer, you already have access to Internet Banking and only need additional access to consult your mother's account. Let me see how we can do that. Please hold. I'll be right back.

From afar, I see Mr. Andrade heading toward me and fixing me with an impenetrable jerk face. The call time was already over 45 minutes. He was going to force me to end the call. And if he found out that I had gone to the branch to get a customer's data, God only knows what would happen to me. My job was on the line, and I still hadn't completely solved Oscar's problem.

With Mr. Andrade's eyes upon me, I gawked dramatically at the window in utter astonishment, as if witnessing a spaceship hovering outside. Unable to resist, he pivoted toward the window to satisfy his curiosity. Seeing nothing out of the ordinary, Mr. Andrade turned back to my desk to find I had magically disappeared.

In the time it had taken him to look, I had locked my screen and crawled under my desk, pulling the chair in close in front of me and trying to make myself invisible, as if my cubicle was empty. Rodrigo, seated in the next cubicle, realized what was happening and sat back to enjoy his front-row seat in my predicament. He unwrapped the chocolate bar Clarice had given him at coffee time and bit unhurriedly into it like someone watching a movie in the cinema, not taking his eyes off the unfolding action.

I could see Mr. Andrade's feet approaching through a crack under my desk. They hesitated a couple of times as he looked around for something until they arrived in front of my cubicle, where they paused momentarily as he asked about my whereabouts.

Rodrigo resurrected the bathroom excuse and embellished it with the suggestion that I must have food poisoning, making unsubstantiated claims about the quality of the Greek barbecue sandwiches sold outside Central Station. By the time he finally left, Mr. Andrade was worried about his own health.

I was so focused on my commitment to solving the customer's problem that, as they talked about bacteria and diarrhea, I took out my phone and googled how Oscar could access his mother's Internet Banking account. From what I'd seen, he would need to obtain a power of attorney through a specific legal process to represent his mother in financial matters. This document is usually called a "Power of Attorney by Private Instrument with Specific Clauses for Management Acts" or simply "Power of Attorney for Banking Matters." This type of power of attorney usually includes specific clauses that authorize the attorney-in-fact (Oscar, in this case) to perform certain acts on behalf of the grantor (his mother) in relation to her bank accounts.

The website I read advised consulting a lawyer or legal professional for precise guidance on how to proceed. I pulled from my pocket the little note that Cesar had written: "Oswald, Legal, eighth floor." My next destination.

I peeked under the table again, but Mr. Andrade's feet were nowhere in sight. I got up slowly, looking around carefully to make sure I wouldn't be discovered.

> Rodrigo: When you meet Mr. Andrade, it would be a good idea to act like you're ill.

He burst out laughing and finished off the last piece of the candy bar. I opened my backpack, grabbed mine, and set off for another leg of my adventure.

> Me: I'll be back.

> Rodrigo: Geez, the guy's completely lost it. Now he doesn't want to stay at his workstation. This is gonna be a total trainwreck...

Running up five flights of stairs was much more tiring than I expected. I felt the weight of my physical unfitness and remembered the abandoned soccer practice. To make matters worse, there's no air conditioning in the stairwell, unlike the offices. So I arrived sweating profusely and gasping for breath at the Legal Department, asking who Oswald was and saying I had an important message that had to be delivered personally. They pointed me to a middle-aged, bald man seated at a table full of books and staring unblinkingly at a computer. I approached him and offered him the chocolate bar I had received from Clarice.

> Me: Good afternoon, sir. Cesar from the ground-floor branch said that maybe you could help me. I'm in a tricky situation trying to help a client.

He stopped what he was doing without taking his hands off the keyboard, just turning his head. He peered at me over his reading glasses, not entirely understanding what was happening. Without moving a muscle, he dropped his gaze to the chocolate I was offering before returning it to my face with a refined version of, "What on Earth...?" I launched into the narrative and told him as quickly as I could about Mrs. Lima and her son Oscar, the concern about suspicious transactions, and the urgency of having access to this data to solve the problem of our unconscious client.

For a few seconds, there was an uncomfortable silence. I think he needed that time to process the avalanche of information I had dumped on him and realize how atypical this situation was.

> Oswald: If I understand correctly, you want me to help somebody I don't know obtain legal authorization immediately when that usually takes several weeks. And to convince me, you intend to bribe me with a cheap candy bar.

On hearing his calm summary, I felt suddenly humiliated and thought that if there were a hole in the ground, I would be desirous of disappearing into it. I gave a sickly and somewhat chagrined smile.

Me: I wouldn't call chocolate a bribe but a sign of good intent and fellowship.

He finally moved his body and turned toward me. He took a deep breath and picked up the chocolate.

Oswald: Very well, then.

He rotated back to his computer and started searching for the relevant files.

Oswald: As the client is unconscious, to be able to act as a temporary legal representative her son needs to present a medical certificate proving her temporary incapacity. He will also need to provide a certified copy of his and his mother's identification documents and a letter from the hospital confirming the admission. I'll give you a document template to share with him. If I get the documentation before 4:30 p.m., I can put the information into the Firms and Powers system, and he will have access to his mother's account.

Me: Can it be a digital copy?

Oswald: Not a chance. A physical document with a notarized signature.

I looked at the clock, and it was 3 p.m. I ran about ten steps toward the stairs and realized I had forgotten something. I stopped and ran back to Oswald's desk.

Me: Thank you. I'll be back here before 4:30 p.m.

Oswald: You do that, young man! But be careful not to have a heart attack and join your client in the hospital.

At that, his serious countenance was transformed. He laughed suddenly and began to eat the chocolate. But before he had taken the first bite, I was already walking briskly down the stairs. Going down is much easier than going up.

On the way from the eighth floor to my workstation, I called a trusted courier who had solved several problems for me before and who, luckily, was available. I asked him to go to the hospital where Mrs. Lima had been admitted and look for her son to collect the documents, take them to the notary office to notarize his signature, and immediately bring them to me.

Arriving at my desk somewhat out of breath, I turned the system back on and hoped Oscar hadn't given up. But he was still there, unwavering, on the other end of the line as he sat in the hospital waiting room, ready for news from me and from the doctors about his mother's condition.

Rodrigo looked a little alarmed at my sweaty, breathless appearance. He pointed silently to my water bottle, most likely in the sage suggestion that I recompose and hydrate myself. I ignored it, of course, because I was too focused on what needed to be done.

Me: Oscar, I'm back. Are you there?

Oscar: Yes. Did you find anything out?

Me: Yes, but we'll have to be quick to get it done today. If I email you some documents, can you edit and print them there at the hospital?

Oscar: Absolutely. I'll ask for help from the nurses, the reception staff, the administration—whoever I can.

Me: You'll need it. You have to obtain some documents from the hospital proving your mother's admission, a certificate from her doctor indicating her incapacity at this time, and a copy of your and your mother's documents. I have already sent a courier to pick these documents up from you. Tell him where the notary office with your registered signature is, so that he can get your signature notarized. Apart from that, I need just one little thing...

Oscar: Of course, what?

Me: I'm sorry, but I need you to pay the courier because I can't afford to.

Oscar: Isn't the courier a service offered by the bank?

Me: No. He's a person I trust.

It was only then that Oscar understood how far I was sticking my neck out to help him. Nothing I had done up to that point was in the manual—there was nothing that could be done. I could easily lose my job, and it would probably even be fair for me to lose it, considering the numerous deviations I was taking to do something that was not only unauthorized but would worsen my department's performance indicators. Our complicity increased further.

Oscar: Don't worry, I'll pay him.

Me: I need to close this call now, but I'll wait for the

courier to arrive here before 4:30 p.m. with your documents to file a legal report and give you access. I'll give you my personal phone number, and you can call me if you have any problems. I've written down your number, and I'll let you know as soon as access is granted so we can check those suspicious transactions together. You can count on me.

I ended the call in the system and took a few minutes to re-establish my heart rhythm. Finally, I drank a gulp of water, looked at the clock, and thought, "If there's a line at the notary's office, there won't be time."

Chapter 4: The Mysterious Transactions

As I answered other calls that afternoon, I couldn't stop thinking about what Oscar was going through. At that moment, he must be running through the hospital corridors, trying to talk to people from different departments and get the documents together. I know that hospitals are as complex and bureaucratic as banks. He would have to convince doctors, nurses, and administrative staff to issue reports and certificates and print documents at the drop of a hat for the motorcycle courier, who was already on his way.

Luckily, my other calls weren't as complex. I did my best to attend to everyone without having to refer anyone to the branch or drop the call without answering their inquiry.

> Customer 2: I need to unblock the credit card I received at home.

> Customer 3: I would like to know what documents I need to apply for a home loan.

Customer 4: I don't know how to put my electricity bill on direct debit through the bank's app.

Nothing was too complicated, and even for those little things I didn't know how to do, I could look up the answer in the bank's product documentation or find someone in the second-level service who could help me sort it out over the phone.

I didn't see Mr. Andrade walking around anymore that day. I wondered if he had noticed the length of my call with Oscar and if I would be punished. It would be worse if the call got caught in the fine net of the audit and they checked the audio of the recording. I couldn't lie. It was all recorded.

Between one call and another, I received messages on my phone informing me that the motorcycle courier had arrived at the hospital, that the documentation had been collected, that the courier was in line to have his signature recognized at the notary's office, that the line was long, that the courier was leaving the office...

It was 4:32 p.m. when the motorcycle courier arrived at the door of the building to give me the documents.

Courier: I'm sorry, but there was a line at the notary's office. I went as fast as I could.

I'm sure he had done his absolute best. It was amazing that those documents had got back to me so quickly. But the deadline had already passed. Oswald had told me to deliver them before 4:30 p.m. I grabbed the documents and took the elevator straight to the eighth floor. This time, I took a chance because I didn't have time to climb eight flights of stairs.

Luckily, the elevator was empty.

Entering the Legal Department, I saw Oswald talking to someone at his desk. "Damn it! He won't be able to see me," I thought desperately. Keeping a respectful distance, I stopped within his range of vision and pointed to the envelope with the documents in it. He excused himself from the conversation, got up, and, with a serious expression, came over to where I was waiting.

> Oswald: It's 4:35 p.m. You're late.

> Me: I'm sorry. There was a line at the notary's office. Would it still be possible to release that access today?

> Oswald: I don't know. How many candy bars do you have left there?

Not knowing what to say, I began patting my empty pockets in the hope that something would miraculously materialize. He noticed my expression of despair and burst out laughing.

> Oswald: I'm teasing you, young man.

He took the envelope from my hand and glanced through the documents to ensure all the information, signatures, and stamps were there. From his rapid appraising glances, you could tell he was an old hand and knew exactly what he was doing.

> Oswald: Tell the client to access the app in about 15 minutes with his username but his mother's branch and account number.

> Me: Thank you.

Oswald: Not at all. I hope his mother makes a speedy recovery.

With that, he turned around and went back to his job. I must admit that my prejudice against the Legal Department had been unfounded. The helpful and agile reception I had received from Oswald was far beyond my expectations. Although I had done everything possible to deliver the documents on time, I hadn't held out much hope of getting access for Oscar that day. I felt triumphant and hugely satisfied. "Sometimes we need to forget common sense and reach for the impossible," I thought, making a mental note of the lesson learned.

I forwarded the excellent news to Oscar by text, and I heard back from him when I was already on my way home.

Oscar: I managed to access the account and find the suspicious transactions, but I don't know how to identify the source.

Me: What appears on the statement?

Oscar: There are two deposits of twenty-plus thousand each.

Me: Deposits? Don't you mean withdrawals?

Oscar: No, deposits. She has a balance of more than 50 thousand in her checking account.

I was confused. Mrs. Maria Lima had a seizure and ended up in the hospital unconscious because there had been too much money in her account. I wish I could get a fright like that! It would be a dream, not a nightmare.

Oscar: The deposits were made today with the codes INV-30014-LQD and INV-30015-LQD. What does that mean?

Each banking transaction on the statement is linked to a source event recorded in the system. These events have identifiers and codes on the statement that allow you to trace the operations. Usually, codes with letters and numbers like these are made up of mnemonics that reveal what they refer to.

Me: Codes that start with INV are related to investments. I would guess that the ending LQD concerns liquidation. Suppose your mother is a shareholder of a fixed-term investment fund. It may be that the deadline expired today, there was automatic liquidation, and the funds were distributed to the shareholders according to their participation.

Oscar: I'll look at the investment statement.

Me: If that's what it is, the money in the checking account was already hers. It was just invested in a fund that ended and returned to her account.

Oscar consulted the statement and confirmed it was the case. The mystery was solved, and he had nothing to worry about. His mother had not been the victim of deception, except perhaps by her own memory and excessive worry. He could reinvest the money or use it as he saw fit.

Oscar: I don't know how to thank you.

Me: You don't have to. I was just doing my job.

Oscar: You've done a lot more than that. With everything that has happened today, I didn't even have time to introduce myself properly, but I'm also a bank employee. I started a short time ago, but I've already noticed how challenging it is to accomplish tasks amidst the bureaucracy there.

"Oscar works for the same company as me!" This was a surprise. That's why he said he had a "strong relationship" with the bank. It was a working relationship.

Me: I tried to do what I thought anyone with a mission to serve a customer should do: solve your problem. I feel great knowing that we got all the information you needed. Now I just hope your mom gets better soon.

Oscar: Thank you. The first results have already come out and ruled out any possibility of stroke or brain damage. That's good news. Doctors have said her condition is stable and are doing additional tests. I'm going to spend the night here, but I'll be back at work tomorrow and not far from the Call Center. Let me at least buy you a coffee and meet you in person. We made a good team today.

Me: Absolutely. It'll be a pleasure.

I hadn't expected this. Oscar and I built a partnership to solve Mrs. Maria Lima's problem, and this partnership could extend beyond a service call. I had found a co-worker and possibly a friend. We arranged to meet at the coffee shop opposite the executive block after lunch for a chat.

After hanging up, I realized I hadn't even asked him what sector he worked in. I remembered the support I had received from my soccer buddy, Cesar, at the branch and the help from Oswald from the Legal Department. I thought about how important it is to create relationships and engage people with a purpose to get results collaboratively. "It's impossible to solve complex problems alone," I thought. I added this to the mental list of lessons learned.

Chapter 5: Another Kind of Coffee

The following morning, I woke up with more energy than usual. Doing something good had made me feel alive. Maybe it was also because of the temperature change. The day dawned cooler as a cold front moved across the city. I didn't even miss the air conditioning at night and could get dressed comfortably without immediately breaking a sweat.

As I pressed the chunks of chilly butter into the bread to have with a mug of milky coffee, I thought about Rodrigo's scrambled eggs with mushrooms and chives. "I'll have to try that one day. It must be good. That guy knows his stuff!"

I went down in the elevator hoping to run into the pretty girl from the sixth floor, but there was no sign of her that day. Maybe there was a hint of perfume in the elevator, but I think it was just my imagination.

On the subway, I didn't have to buy tickets that day because I already had them, and I went straight to the sardine compression chamber for my jolting journey to Central Station.

On the way, I thought about my work. Something had changed in me the day before. How was I going to act from then on? Would I continue with my commitment to generate results, no matter the cost, to feel motivated and happy with myself? Would that be sustainable? Or would I lose my job when they found out that the department's goals were being neglected? It would be much easier to just go with the flow and accomplish my tasks without question. But is that what I wanted to do with my life?

As I passed the lady playing the toy guitar, I stopped for a moment:

Let life take me; life takes me…

I thought for a moment about the lyrics of the song and how they applied to my own life. I didn't want to let life take me anymore. I couldn't carry on with the same resigned behavior I'd always had, playing a supporting role in my own life. I wanted to be the protagonist. I wanted to decide my own fate, not depend on the mercy of chance. But how do you do that? How could I change a system I couldn't control? These questions were suffocating me. Perhaps letting life take me was about not being simply a leaf in the wind but a sailor using the currents of air and water to navigate, embracing life's opportunities with gratitude and proactivity.

I am happy and grateful for all that God gave me.

I don't usually give money away. I see many people downtown asking for money, and I think, over time, I've become a little hard-hearted. Unfeeling. But that day, I felt like giving some money to the old lady who had afforded me these reflections.

I opened my wallet and found it was empty. There were no coins in the coin compartment. I explored the space behind my ID and found a ten-dollar bill carefully folded and flattened out of sight. "Dona Rosa's[3] good luck charm!" I remembered that many years ago, I had promised to give this money to someone in need. I took it out of my wallet and put it in the little box in front of the old lady without unfolding it. If I remember correctly, the bill held some seeds that were part of the charm. I didn't want them to fall out. The old lady looked at me, smiled without missing a beat on the strings of the little guitar, and we sang together.

> Let life take me; life takes me...
> I am happy and grateful for all that God gave me.

I entered the bank premises, waved my card at the turnstile sensor, clocked in, and went up to the third floor to my workstation. I had barely sat down when I turned, startled, to see Mr. Andrade leaning against my cubicle. This was the moment I had been dreading. I had escaped him the day before—now, it was time to face reality. My insubordination would not go unpunished.

Me: Good morning, Mr. Andrade.

Mr. Andrade: Good morning. Are you better?

Me: Am I better?

Mr. Andrade: I was worried about you. Food poisoning can be serious.

---

3. "Dona" is a respectful title used in Portuguese, similar to "Mrs." or "Madam" in English. It's often used to address more mature women.

Me: Oh! Yes. I'm better. Yesterday, I felt awful, but I'm feeling much better today. Thank you.

Mr. Andrade: You need to be careful. Young people think they can eat whatever they like and nothing can hurt them, but that's not true. Be careful of the kind of street food you eat. Stay away from fried food and dirty stalls. Try to eat homemade food whenever you can.

Me: Yes, sir. I'll do that.

Once again, I was surprised. While I was expecting dismissal or punishment for disrupting the indicators that could give this man a bonus, he was concerned about my well-being and took his time to give me some advice. I felt strangely touched and relieved. That time, I had got away with it. In the next cubicle, my accomplice laughed and teased me.

Rodrigo: You really have to stop eating that Greek barbecue from Central Station.

Me: I owe you one.

...

Work in the morning went smoothly, and I didn't have any major difficulties. I tried my best to help the customers who needed it, and I was successful in practically every case. A simple change of attitude had made my work more meaningful and pleasurable, generating value for customers and the company. I no longer felt that long-standing frustration, although I could see many areas where we could improve. "Someone really should take a look at these processes and systems," I thought. "But until things get an upgrade, we'll do the best we can."

The morning went by quickly, and at the agreed time, I went to the coffee shop in front of the executive block to meet Oscar. At the table he had indicated, a well-dressed gentleman with graying hair was drinking coffee and reading something on his phone.

Me: Oscar?

Oscar: Yes. It's me.

Interesting! I had imagined him younger. His voice was so full of energy and life. Not that his appearance contradicted that—quite the opposite. He was middle-aged, lean, and elegant, both in physique and manner—the image of a successful person. He motioned to the waiter and ordered another coffee.

Oscar: Thank you for coming here and for the support you gave me yesterday.

Me: My pleasure. How's your mom?

Oscar: Much better. She's already conscious and out of danger. Apparently, she suffered a drop in blood pressure due to hypoglycemia. She has diabetes. With this concern about the "suspicious transactions," she forgot to eat at her regular time. She passed out, hitting her head as she fell, and was unconscious for quite some time. But, according to the doctor, it's nothing serious, and she'll be fine. She's under observation for another day because of the head injury, but I think she'll be back home tonight.

Me: What a scare!

Oscar: Absolutely. I told her she needs to be careful and eat properly.

I remembered Mr. Andrade's advice. It was funny that my fake eating problem from the day before had been caused by the real eating problem of the person I was helping.

The waiter brought the coffee, and when I tried it, I thought, "My God, that's good! So that's what coffee should taste like." It was very different from the dirty water at the Call Center. "I need to bring Rodrigo to this place one day. He'll love it."

Oscar wanted to know more about me, including my age, education, where I came from, and how long I had worked at the bank. Listing his questions makes it sound like an interview, but that's not how I felt. It was a relaxed and friendly chat with someone kind who showed interest.

He wanted to know more about the previous day. I told him about my run to the branch, hiding under the table, the Internet search on types of power of attorney, the suffocating stairwell, and the chocolate to win over the legal expert. He was amused to hear the whole history that he was also a part of from a different point of view.

Oscar: On the other end of the line, we have no idea what's happening. Internal customer service processes are like a big black box with an entrance to place an order and an exit on the other side where something is expected to be delivered properly. I'm glad to hear your story and know that some people care.

Me: Everyone should care.

Oscar: Absolutely, but I know that's not the standard around here. I've only been with the company for six months, but I've already realized that the corporate culture differs from that. You are an outlier.

I felt uncomfortable, but I couldn't disagree with him. The majority of people work to do, at most, the least. The company delivers little and costs too much, and everyone pretends otherwise. No one dares to speak ill of the company's processes, products, systems, or culture at formal events. It looks like we're perfect.

Our company is an example to be followed.

I'm proud to be part of this team.

But what you hear on the grapevine, in the cafes and corridors where the conversation is more candid and personal, is entirely different.

Me: Working just to get paid is frustrating. I would like to work for a higher purpose.

Oscar smiled with an expression of contentment as if an expectation was confirmed at that moment.

Oscar: Come with me to my department. I want to tell you a little about what I'm doing and make you a proposal.

I was curious and a little apprehensive. What kind of proposal? What hot water might I be getting myself into? I looked at the clock and saw that my lunch break was almost over.

Me: Thanks for the invitation, but we'll have to leave it for another time. My lunch hour is almost up. I need to get back and clock in.

Oscar: Consider yourself back. Don't worry. I'll sort it out with Mr. Andrade later.

I didn't get it. "What does he mean he'll sort it out with Mr. Andrade? Do they know each other? Are they friends?" Not knowing what to do, I went with the flow. "Let life take me," I thought.

He paid the bill and led the way across the street and into the office block on the opposite side of the street. It was the most beautiful of the buildings in which the bank had offices, very different from the Call Center block, which is like an industrial warehouse staffed by faceless people. I had already been in the reception a few times to gaze at the architecture and the dazzling Christmas decorations, although I had never gone beyond that point. I was worried my card wouldn't work at the turnstiles there, but I didn't need it. Oscar motioned to the security guard, who opened the side access so we could enter without going through the turnstiles.

Security: Good afternoon, sir.

Oscar: Good afternoon. This young man is with me.

We ascended to the thirteenth floor in a mirror-lined elevator with a small television that displayed that month's birthdays. The architecture and decoration on this floor were even more elegant than the reception. Wood and leather furniture was arranged around a private reception, and fresh flowers were on the pretty receptionist's countertop. She wished us good afternoon with a smile as we entered an executive room with a name on the door:

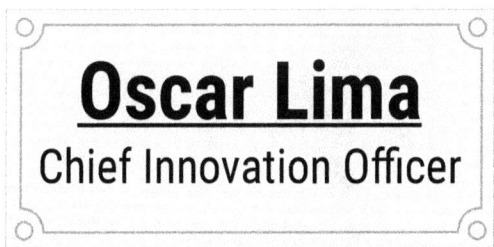

Oscar Lima
Chief Innovation Officer

Chapter 6: Outputs and Outcomes

We made small talk from the coffee shop to the room in the Executive Block, and I tried to hide how awestruck I was to be there. I would never have thought that Oscar was one of the bank's directors. State Bank directors are like Hollywood stars. You only see them in newspapers or on TV. It's quite beyond belief to be in a cafe having a friendly chat with one of them, let alone hearing them ask about your life with genuine interest. I realized afterward that I had got it the wrong way around. "What an idiot!" I thought. "I should have been asking about his life." But the big question I was almost bursting to know was, "What plans does he have for me?"

Oscar: Do you know the difference between outputs and outcomes?

Me: I'm not sure I do. I never really thought about it before.

Oscar: Okay, let me explain with an example. Think of a service provider that will offer a service to a customer. Anything that comes to mind.

Me: An auto repair shop?

Oscar: Perfect. An auto repair shop.

God, what I'd give to have a car! I should have suggested something else, but it's too late now. I had better go with it.

Oscar: You go to the mechanic to have your car's suspension changed. He tells you the price, and you agree to pay for the parts plus the service. In the end, he gives you the car with the suspension changed and an invoice showing how much to pay. You didn't even see him do it, but you know he did because you received the work delivery. You made a request and left with the suspension changed and an invoice.

Me: Input and output.

Oscar: Exactly. The output is what the service provider delivers to the customer. But in this case, suppose you weren't satisfied and came back complaining that the car keeps making the same noise as before. The mechanic doesn't understand why you're dissatisfied. He delivered exactly what you had agreed on: replacing the suspension. So, what are you complaining about?

Me: From what I can see, I didn't want to replace the suspension. I wanted the car to stop making noise.

Oscar: That's right. Replacing the suspension didn't yield the result you were hoping for. This result that the customer perceives is what we call the outcome.

I didn't understand where he was going with this or what the story of output and outcome had to do with me, but I thought it best to follow his train of thought and try to learn something.

Me: Okay, so let me get this straight. Output is what the provider delivers, and the outcome is what the customer actually wants.

Oscar: Well, there may be a difference between desire and reality. The outcome is the result, but it isn't always exactly what the customer expects. It might even be very different from what they would like. While the output is what was physically produced by the provider's task, the outcome is the consequence. Understanding the consequence goes far beyond the provider's perspective alone. In general, how do you think you should evaluate the quality of a product or service?

Me: Quality? That's a treacherous word! Quality depends on your point of view. I might think the coffee shop we visited today is excellent, but someone else might think it's not that good because they had different expectations.

Oscar: You're right. Different authors define quality in different ways. Many claim that quality should be a measure of conformity to a specification to avoid this personal bias and allow for accurate measurement. For example, coffee from the coffee shop should be delivered in a maximum of two minutes, at a temperature of 70°C, with a maximum variation of five degrees up or down, in a porcelain cup, in the amount of 50ml—something quite specific.

Me: Okay. I can understand this logic of quality based on specifications and detailed measurements, but what if the customer doesn't care about any of that? What if, for them, the vital thing in a coffee shop is to have a nice place to chat with a friend?

Oscar: Good question! If something doesn't add value, it doesn't make a difference to the quality. That's why the specification we use to measure quality can't be made with a focus only on the output. If we want to measure quality, we have to evaluate the outcome. There's no point in saying it conforms to the specification if the customer is dissatisfied.

Me: At the auto repair shop, the mechanic replaced the suspension, but the noise continued to bother the customer. So, it wasn't good service.

I started to relate the difference between output and outcome to my work and saw that it had everything to do with the call with Oscar. Initially, he had just asked for an insurance policy number, but his need was much more complex than that. What he needed was to enable the insurance coverage to admit his mother to the hospital, investigate the suspicious financial transactions in her account, and take the necessary actions in case of fraud. And he needed it all to be done urgently.

In most calls, our Call Center agents don't put much effort into understanding the expected outcome. Putting yourself in other people's shoes and understanding their real needs is too much hassle. The goal imposed on us was to give a quick response, generate the output, and move on to the next call, even if the answer was to tell the customer to go to their local branch without solving their problem.

> Me: To understand the outcome, you must put yourself in the customer's position.

> Oscar: More than that. It requires an even broader view. The result has consequences for the customer but not for the customer alone. Others will also be affected. Shareholders, employees, the government, and the environment.

> Me: What do you mean? Isn't making the customer happy the mission of every company?

> Oscar: Customer satisfaction is an essential measure of success for evaluating quality, but not the only one. Was the result good for the business? Did it make a profit? Are the employees happy? Did we pay the tax? Did we avoid polluting nature? A business that pleases the customer but leaves a trail of blood along the way is not sustainable.

I immediately thought of a drug dealer's business, but then I understood that he was using "trail of blood" as a metaphor. And it made a lot of sense for any organization. A business can't last long if it doesn't cater to all these impacted stakeholders beyond the customer. It may keep going for a while, but if it doesn't have outcomes that meet their expectations, the business will eventually fall apart.

> Me: I think I understand the difference between output and outcome. In my case at the Call Center, the answers

I give to the customer and the information I record in the system during a call are just the outputs of my work. Outcomes relate to how it helped the customer solve their problem and how it helped the bank build customer loyalty, make money, and avoid risks.

Oscar: Precisely! You've got it. This concept is fundamental to my area here at the bank, which is innovation. Let me tell you a bit about my challenge here.

Oscar said that, before working at the bank, he was CEO of a very successful technology startup that ended up being considered a unicorn, which is the name they give to very innovative companies that gain a billionaire valuation quickly. His success attracted the attention of the bank's board, who urgently sought to innovate and hired him to carry out a significant company transformation.

For the last six months, he had been trying to bring about meaningful change, but he was finding it hard. As part of the strategy to become more innovative, the bank had already bought three cutting-edge startups. It incorporated these companies into its structure to launch new products, but none took off. In the end, as soon as the new companies were incorporated, they also became slow and bureaucratic. I wasn't surprised.

Me: The culture here at the bank is pervasive. Everyone is output-driven and couldn't care less about outcomes. I think that's typical of big companies. People lose sight of the whole and just take care of their patch.

Oscar: True. Peter Drucker once said, "Culture eats

strategy for breakfast."[4] After six months, I've come to the conclusion that we need to transform the corporate culture to make any impact. New technology or product launches won't make the company innovative. In fact, the introduction of new technologies won't make much difference at all.

Me: Can't a new product be considered an innovation?

Oscar: It could be, but it's just a quick fix. Once the product is launched, the novelty wears off and it becomes routine. Being an innovative company requires constant creativity. To innovate, we use the available resources to generate more and more value. To generate value, we need an outcome-driven culture. My challenge is to change the bank's culture.

Me: Man, that's tough! Changing the bank's culture makes the twelve labors of Hercules look like a walk in the park. It's a huge challenge. How are you going to do it?

Oscar: I'll need help. Which is why you're here. Would you like to work with me?

If this were a sitcom, it would be the moment I spat my drink out in a fountain of astonishment. I had thought Oscar might have a proposal for me, but I didn't expect it to be such an impossible task.

---

4. According to the Drucker Institute, Peter Drucker never said, "Culture eats strategy for breakfast." What he did say, in his article for *The Wall Street Journal* (March 28, 1991) was that "culture—no matter how defined—is singularly persistent." Much more nuanced and certainly less sexy.

Chapter 7: The Proposal

I couldn't quite figure out what had led Oscar to pick me to help him transform the bank's corporate culture. He must have been desperate. After all, I had absolutely no experience in the area or proper training—I'm just a call center agent.

> Oscar: The way you treated me yesterday was a far cry from the standard culture I see around here. You weren't just attending to outputs. You made a point of understanding what my mother and I needed and spared no effort to find solutions to our problems. You overcame every obstacle, sought help internally in other areas, and even outsourced a courier. Those are the actions of an innovative person. You have the profile I want to replicate in the bank. And that's the most important thing to me.

Could it be true? Oscar had no idea how atypical his call was in my professional life. It was just some random decision, over coffee with Rodrigo, to go to any length to solve the problem of the next customer who called. I had made a kind of bet with myself to make the day more exciting. Deep down, I'm not like that. It was just a one-off event.

An atypical behavior of mine had deceived Oscar. That person who helped him yesterday wasn't the real me. It was just a simulation—a fake. I hadn't even heard of outputs and outcomes before. I was an ordinary, unadventurous, stuck-in-a-rut kind of guy. He needed someone much more able and committed.

> Me: I'm sorry, Oscar, but I wouldn't know where to start with this cultural transformation. I'm just a call center agent.

> Oscar: You're modest. That's another good thing about you. Knowing that you don't know something is an excellent place to start. Before hiring me, the bank hired some of the largest management consultancies, who knew exactly what was needed to make the bank more innovative. They brought the so-called "best practices." They implemented a set of standardized frameworks and ways of working models with structured processes, well-defined roles and responsibilities, and templates for innovation that would need to be created with the most modern techniques... Do you know what the result was?

> Me: Everyone working in their own little box to deliver their outputs?

> Oscar: Exactly. They changed the processes, but they didn't change the culture. Ultimately, the bank made a handsome investment for everything to stay exactly the same. It was a tremendous waste.

Me: But what could I do? I don't know anything about innovation or organizational transformation.

Oscar: You know how to listen to customers, understand their needs, and look for valuable results. You act the way the bank needs everyone to behave. We need to contaminate everyone with this attitude of yours. It doesn't matter that we don't yet know how we're going to do it. We can find out together—if you accept my offer, of course.

At that moment, my response to his offer was overshadowed by a foreboding sense of disaster waiting to happen. Leave a stable, secure position for this Mission Impossible? Maybe if I was a hotshot like Tom Cruise. Unfortunately, the most likely conclusion was that Oscar would get the same result as the previous consultancies and wouldn't last long in the company. Why would I buy into this suicide pact? What's in it for me?

He anticipated my unspoken question with a distinctly discouraging disclosure: he didn't yet have a definition or salary for the new position that I would assume. It's not something that's ever existed before. At first, I would just be "borrowed" from the Call Center to work in the Innovation Department without any change in my contract. That is, with the same salary and working hours. Based on the results obtained in the first few weeks, we could define a more structured proposal but no promises.

Me: It sounds a bit risky, Oscar.

Oscar: Everyone is at risk, but not everyone is aware. Do you know why the State Bank needs to invest in innovation?

I figured it was a rhetorical question and made an appropriately curious face while waiting for a generic textbook answer, but the reason he gave surprised me. It was much more tangible and specific than I could have imagined.

Oscar: Everybody's job here at the bank is at risk. You may have noticed that the market has changed significantly in recent years. Before, only four or five banks dominated the national financial market. Each specialized in a specific target audience or had a greater presence in some regions of the country with very little competition. Today, hundreds of small fintech companies offer cheaper, higher quality products and services than large banks. In addition, there are international companies that operate remotely. Access to services over the Internet has made most of the banks' physical branches obsolete. That's a very high cost to maintain, which makes us less competitive.

Me: And we keep telling people to go and solve their problems at their local branch, which nobody wants to do.

Oscar: See how we're being overtaken? Many customers are migrating to other providers. And that's just one side of it. From a shareholder perspective, much of the investment money is being migrated to different businesses with higher return potential. From the point of view of internal talent, most of the employees with more experience have already left the bank to work in another location that offers better conditions. We're losing on all sides.

Me: Good heavens! I didn't realize it was that serious.

Oscar: But it is. The bank takes a long time to sense and respond to changes in the market. If it doesn't change, it won't survive.

I was shocked by the assertion that the State Bank could cease to exist. It seemed so stable and eternal—it had never crossed my mind that it could fail. But come to think of it, it's possible and maybe even probable. Before it was privatized a few decades ago, the bank had been state-owned, when much of its bureaucratic culture was formed. Today, it's a private company and must compete in the marketplace. It will only survive if it offers superior quality service.

Me: I don't know what to say.

Oscar: Of course. You don't have to answer me now. Go home early today and think about whether you want to join my team. I don't want to pressure you. It has to be your decision. This will only make sense if you're committed to the outcomes we're pursuing. You have my phone number, and you can call me if you have any questions. Or come to my office whenever you want. Just don't take too long to make up your mind. We have a lot to do.

I said goodbye to Oscar and thanked him for the coffee and the conversation. I left his office with a dry mouth and the beginnings of a belly ache. On the way to the elevator and then walking through the reception, I admired once again the architecture and beautiful decoration of the Executive Block. I thought about the fragility of everything threatened by smaller and more innovative competing companies that probably didn't have these maintenance costs and were much more aligned with the outcomes expected by the market.

Who was I to make an impact in this situation? I couldn't help Oscar with that. Poor guy! But the most disturbing thing was realizing that even if I didn't accept the proposal and stayed in the Call Center, there was no stability for me or anyone else. The whole bank was in danger. "I think I need to update my resume," I thought, "and take something for this stomachache. It's killing me."

Chapter 8: The Little Bird and the Egg

The subway on the way home rattled my body, but my mind was somewhere else, detached from me. It was a little earlier than my usual rush-hour journey, and the train was less crowded. I even managed to sit down. My head spun with thoughts of outputs and outcomes, people working in cafes and auto repair shops, some committed to results and others merely worrying about their own lives. I wondered what would become of mine. I felt exhausted. Like I'd just run a marathon. My body felt like lead. I didn't realize that thinking consumed so much energy.

I lost track of time and almost missed my stop. Fortunately, a familiar face at the station roused me from my trance, and I hopped off the train in time. It was the pretty girl from the sixth floor. She was on the same train and must have been on her way home too. I quickened my pace and managed to get closer, at which point she recognized me and offered the same polite smile and greeting as when I had met her at the elevator door. "Good afternoon," she said.

I was glad she acknowledged me instead of pretending not to see me, like so many other neighbors do. She didn't treat me like a stranger but as someone to be trusted. I immediately forgot about my dilemmas, and my mood changed completely. She was dressed sensibly—a white buttoned shirt, a gray skirt, and flat sandals, which only accentuated her beauty and sensuality. She was carrying a backpack with the emblem of a well-known school downtown. We knew we were going to the same address and set off together. I tried to fill the uncomfortable silence and asked her name. "Julia," she said.

Me: Do you go to this school?

I pointed to the backpack, trying to strike up a conversation.

Julia: No. I'm a preschool assistant teacher. I take care of the very little ones.

"God, what an idiot! Of course, she doesn't go to school," I thought. "She's not a child anymore. Why do I ask these moronic questions?"

Julia: What about you? What do you do?

Me: I work at the State Bank.

Julia: In a branch?

Me: No. At the head office. In the Call Center.

I stumbled over my words slightly in answering because my situation suddenly seemed much less stable than it had that morning. How long would I still be working at the bank? How long would the bank even continue to exist? Should I accept the Innovation Department offer? Or should I start sending out my resume? The mental confusion wanted to come back, but I blinked hard and focused on Julia to escape my anxiety and thoughts about work.

Me: Is it nice working in a school?

Julia: That depends on what you consider nice. The salary's a pittance, and it's very hard work, but it's incredibly rewarding.

Julia told me that she had a law degree and had worked in a law firm for a while, but she wasn't happy. She decided to abandon her career as a lawyer and was now finishing a second degree in education in an evening course while interning at the school.

Julia: The purity of children feeds my soul. I keep thinking that each of them is the seed of an adult, and if they're well cultivated, they'll blossom into leaders, innovators, artists, fathers, and mothers who can make a better world. Did you know that the first years of a person's life are the most crucial for their intellectual and moral development? I'm honored to share the most critical mission a person could have. I am a horticulturist in the garden of tomorrow's minds.

The poetic way that she saw her profession was moving. She didn't go to work merely to earn money in exchange for a day's toil and the activities it entailed. Money was by no means the motivating factor. She could be earning a lot more as a lawyer. What fulfilled her was making a positive impact on the world, one that might only be fully realized decades later. She would receive no thanks for it and probably wouldn't even be remembered, although her influence would be engraved on her students' way of thinking, feeling, and acting.

Me: That's a beautiful way to see your work.

Julia: I don't know how to see it any other way. It's the only one that makes sense to me.

On entering the building, she asked the doorman if a package had arrived and received a negative response. I wondered if it was the same order she had asked about the day before.

Me: Internet shopping?

Julia: Yes. I'm waiting for an order I bought on a Chinese website several weeks ago. It's supposed to be here. I don't know why it's taking so long.

Me: I've bought things on foreign websites that took ages to arrive, too.

We got into the elevator, and when it stopped on the sixth floor, she said goodbye and thanked me for being her companion during the walk.

Me: I live in 805. If you need anything, just call.

Julia: Thanks. I'm in 604. You can count on me, too. Neighbors should be there for each other.

Me: Absolutely!

I arrived home in a calmer state of mind. Thinking about Julia made me feel better. Her sweet manner, pure smile, and romantic view of life intoxicated me. I passed the evening in lighter spirits and slept warmly in love.

The next day, I woke up at the usual time and took a cool shower before getting dressed. With my body temperature lowered, putting on my work clothes was more enjoyable, and I felt more energetic. Something felt different about me. I heard the birds chirping outside and felt inspired.

I grabbed the hard butter from the fridge, carved off a thin slab, and then had a thought. Instead of trying to flatten it onto yesterday's bread like every other day, I melted the butter into a frying pan and placed the two halves of the bread on top. In a minute, the open side of the soft, warmed bread was crisp and buttery. My coffee tasted even better as I sipped it, surrounded by the delicious, toasted aroma. "Why didn't I think of doing this before?" I thought. Simple things that make life so much better and take no time at all. I realized that I had been going through life without savoring it, either because I was too lazy or too stuck in my ways.

At the subway station, it was the same old push-and-shove. But when the train door opened, and the people behind me started pushing to get in, I stepped back off the train and spread my arms like a human barrier, holding the frenzied herd behind me and loudly telling them to wait for the people inside the train to get off first. Among the other passengers, an elderly lady stepped carefully from the train and thanked me as she went past. The people behind got the idea and waited their turn without pushing. No longer swimming against a tide of bodies, we got onto the train calmly and positioned ourselves inside the tin like civilized sardines.

A little later, as I emerged from Central Station, I was struck by a strange emptiness. Something was missing from the landscape, as if they had demolished an old building or cut down an ancient tree. Then I realized what was out of place. Where was the old lady with the toy guitar? The corner on the sidewalk, next to the post office, was empty. I looked around, but I couldn't see her. The familiar street vendors and people hopeful of donations were at their posts, but the guitar lady was nowhere to be seen.

I felt something like a mixture of curiosity, mysticism, and stupidity. Of course, it didn't mean anything. It's not as if she were a fairy godmother in disguise who would change my life just because I had given her some money. Nor had I made any spectacular change to her life. I had maybe bought her a hot meal, if that. And, let's be honest, those little seeds weren't magic beans that would lead her to a giant's castle in the clouds and a goose that lays golden eggs. Who was I kidding? It was just a coincidence that she wasn't there—she'd surely be there the next day. Right?

I arrived at the Call Center with no time to spare and started work with the same determination to solve customer problems as I had in the past two days. Except this time, I was thinking, "What is the expected outcome of this call?" I liked having a word to name the significant results of my work. I felt good. I was excited about my work in a way that I had never been before.

At break time, I caught Rodrigo's eye and nodded toward the door. As we headed for the coffee corner, we met two members of our team. They grimaced and gave us a thumbs down.

> Colleague: Don't bother going to the coffee machine. It's clogged up again. We've already told Mr. Andrade, and he's called General Services. Now we'll have to wait.

Rodrigo: Oh, rats! Last time, it took them three days to show up and clean the filter. Does the coffee suck? Yeah. But that's all we have to give us a little energy in our day—or *had*. Now, we don't even have that.

Me: Can't we clean the filter?

Rodrigo: It's not our job. General Services personnel are responsible.

Me: Okay, but I want to have coffee today. And it's not exactly rocket science. I know the General Services crew, and no one there strikes me as a post-grad in coffee machine maintenance. Let's take a look!

I went to the coffee corner, and Rodrigo followed me curiously.

Rodrigo: You're acting weird. You left early yesterday, and now you're all excited, wanting to fix the coffee machine... Man, what's going on?

While I was examining the coffee machine and figuring out how to clean the filter, I told him about my conversation with Oscar the day before. I told him we had been working driven by outputs, while what really matters are outcomes.

Me: It's like, this machine here makes coffee. But what it generates is much more important than just the coffee. It's responsible for our one moment of relaxation and leisure. The time we exchange ideas and socialize. That's important stuff. Output and outcome are different things.

Rodrigo: It's leaking from that corner.

Me: There we go! I think I've figured out where the filter is.

I turned a screw and removed a part clogged beyond recognition with coffee grounds. Taking care not to make too much of a mess, I slid the wastebasket under the machine and dumped the powdery black lump into the trash. Then I took the part over to the sink and started washing it.

> Me: Just like this machine, the people here at the bank aren't working properly because they're bogged down with a decades-long culture of inefficient bureaucracy, just taking care of their local tasks without thinking about the big picture.

> Rodrigo: Are coffee grounds meant to represent the bank's corporate culture?

I realized I might have stretched the metaphor a bit too far.

> Me: I mean, the Innovation Department's challenge is to make the company work properly. And to do that, you need to make people commit to outcomes, not outputs. That's not easy! People don't even know what the expected outcomes of their work are, and even if they did, they don't care. They want to earn their salary, and that's it.

I put the machine back together, placed a cup under the coffee outlet, and switched it on. The machine heated up and made the coffee with a quieter noise than usual. I gave the first cup to Rodrigo and asked if it had come out okay.

> Rodrigo: Better than before. I don't think anyone has cleaned this thing in years.

Me: Gross.

I got a cup of coffee for myself and signaled to my colleagues that the machine was working.

Me: Oscar made this offer for me to go and work with him, but I don't think I have the right profile. I don't know if I should accept it.

Rodrigo: You're kidding, right? It seems obvious enough to me.

Me: Does it?

Rodrigo: Well, yes. If it were me, I most definitely would not accept.

He threw his empty cup in the trash and raised both arms playfully.

Rodrigo: I'm chasing nothing, and nothing's chasing me. But take a look at you!

Then, he changed his expression and took on a more serious and profound tone, which surprised me. I had never seen Rodrigo speak so earnestly.

Rodrigo: Maybe last week, I could have doubted it, but seeing you today, the way you're serving customers, fixing the coffee machine, and talking to me about these ideas, it's like a little bird that has come out of its egg. There's no turning back. It's you who doesn't fit in the Call Center anymore.

Me: So you think I should accept the proposal?

Rodrigo: I think you've already accepted it. You just haven't admitted it yet.

I paused momentarily to reflect and realized that my friend's words were valid. I didn't want to be ashamed of my work anymore. I didn't want to merely complete tasks in exchange for a salary. I wanted my effort to have meaning. I wanted to make an impact, and the offer to work in the Innovation Department gave me a chance to do so. It didn't even matter what I earned. It was what I wanted to do. I took a sip of coffee.

Me: Praise be, it really is better! And you're right. I'll accept the proposal.

Rodrigo: Fly, little bird! Fly!

Chapter 9: Workshop

Oscar was waiting excitedly for me in his office at the agreed time.

> Oscar: I was pleased to receive your message of acceptance. You won't regret joining the Innovation Department.

He gave me a firm handshake that seemed to seal the deal. He was smiling and ready to get started. He didn't even sit down while we talked.

> Me: When do I start?

> Oscar: Right now!

> Me: But don't I need to transfer from the Call Center to here? And complete the paperwork with HR?

> Oscar: My secretary will take care of that. Don't worry.

Working with Oscar was undoubtedly different from what we were used to at the bank. To clean the coffee machine filter, we needed to open a ticket with General Services and wait three days for someone to show up and do it. Yet Oscar was moving an employee to his area without signing a contract, formalizing the transfer, having a selection process, making a job announcement, or following any defined formal process. What was I getting myself into?

> Me: How am I going to get started today? I'm not even sure what my job is!

> Oscar: Come with me. I'm going to introduce you to someone who can give you some tips on working in an outcome-driven way.

We went straight to the IT Department building. Oscar was going to introduce me to a senior business analyst named Barbara. She was an expert in identifying the expected outcomes of systems development and maintenance projects and ensuring that the people working on those projects were investing their time and effort in what really matters. Along the way, I felt a little insecure because I'm not a tech expert. These IT people seem to speak a language that no one understands except themselves and the computers they interact with more naturally than people.

> Me: I don't understand one thing. Yesterday, you told me that innovation would not come from adopting new technologies. Today, you're taking me to the IT Department.

> Oscar: That's a valid observation. However, your visit here isn't about how to deal with machines but how to deal with people. Barbara also has the behavior we need

to innovate, and she has something extra that is just what you're looking for right now.

Me: Courage?

Oscar burst out laughing!

Oscar: Oh, you have courage. Otherwise, you wouldn't be here. The extra thing Barbara has is method. She has mastered several analysis techniques that help her think clearly and engage people in organizational change.

Me: Is she part of your team?

Oscar: Do you mean *our* team?

With his gaze, he challenged me to assume, once again, my role and accountability for the results. I realized he was gradually involving me with the goals to be reached.

Me: Yes, of course. Our team.

Oscar: Well, yes and no. She's someone I can count on because she's an IT transformation and innovation agent, but I can't take her out of IT to work on corporate culture for the whole organization. She's on several strategic IT projects. If I steal her, the IT director will kill me.

We arrived in a very spacious meeting room. People were coming for the event about to start, and the inviting aroma of freshly brewed coffee welcomed us. In the center of the room stood a large U-shaped table, with a prism inscribed with a participant's name placed in front of each chair. People were taking their seats and chatting, creating a background hum of simultaneous voices. There were people from different departments, and I noticed no prisms with our names on them. It was probably something important, and we hadn't been invited.

Barbara came over as we stood near a small table with a flask of coffee, water, and cookies. She was dressed in modest business attire and must have been close to retirement age. She spoke calmly, and it struck me immediately that she paid careful attention to what people said. Most people want to give their opinions and be heard, but she was the opposite. I couldn't wait for her words of wisdom, but she listened more than she talked.

Oscar introduced us and quickly explained that I needed some tips on where to get started.

> Barbara: It'll be a pleasure to help! But I can't talk right now—we have a product design workshop starting in three minutes. Why don't you hang around and listen in?

> Oscar: Excellent idea! He can get a hands-on view of how a business analyst works.

Barbara showed me to a chair at the back of the room where I could observe the proceedings, and I settled in. Oscar thanked her and then excused himself.

> Oscar: You're in good hands. We'll talk later.

I hadn't felt so utterly out of place in an eternity. I had an unsettling flashback to starting a new school as a kid. The first day was horrendous, and I cried so much that the teacher was at a loss for what to do with me. I remembered despondently that it had taken me a good few days to adapt and start making friends. Luckily, right on cue, Barbara cleared her throat and teleported me instantaneously back to the grown-up me in a professional environment. I adjusted my tie and blinked hard. This was big school.

Barbara opened the meeting by asking the participants at the U-shaped table to introduce themselves. I saw that they all held at least one managerial position. Barbara introduced me and the other two observers at the back. I was from the Innovation Department studying the process of creating products, and the other two guys were system developers for the product being defined in the meeting.

It was an important meeting where the Marketing team was urgently calling for the creation of a lead system and outlining how it should work. In marketing and sales, a lead is a business opportunity in which the customer shows interest in a product or service, shares some personal data, and would likely welcome further contact at an appropriate time.

The atmosphere was less than cordial. While Marketing and Sales seemed desperate to get the system up and running quickly, the IT and Operations teams, who define how things work in the branches, seemed reluctant and disagreed with the functionalities proposed for the new system. The meeting looked unlikely to produce an agreement until Barbara changed her approach.

> Barbara: Let's take a step back and better understand the needs to be met before focusing on product design.

Marketing Director: What for? I can't see the point in going backward when we have no time to waste.

Barbara: That's understandable, but if you could bear with me, I need your help. You see, I don't know what you're all thinking, and I won't be able to help you without understanding the context. So, first of all, what problem do we want to solve?

Marketing Director: Building a lead system.

Barbara: That's unlikely to be the root of the problem. It's probably a solution for a more profound need. Why do we need a lead system?

The marketing director seemed a little impatient, but he embarked on the challenge of answering the facilitator's questions.

Marketing Director: We need a lead system to access information about business opportunities.

Barbara: And why do we need the information about business opportunities?

Marketing Director: To be able to follow up with interested potential customers.

Barbara: Why?

Marketing Director: To increase sales, our company's revenue, and profit.

Although the exchange wasn't exactly amicable, the director ended up listing the goals of the very initiative Barbara wanted to bring to light. I realized with satisfaction that I understood what she was doing. She was looking to identify the expected outcomes of that initiative using a technique that I later learned is called "The Five Whys." This technique consists of asking "why" until you get to the root of a problem. Although the method mentions five "whys," the number five is not necessarily the magic number. You can repeat the question as many times as necessary.

Barbara: Okay, that's Marketing's vision. What other issues are we dealing with here?

Now that she had clarified the vision of the Marketing Department's goals, she looked at other visions to create a bigger picture of the context.

IT Manager: Our development team is overallocated with projects already underway. Getting these two developers here as observers was already a sacrifice. We can't produce a new system within the timeframe expected by Marketing without working overtime and outsourcing developers. That's an additional cost that IT can't absorb.

Operations Manager: Branch personnel are also already overwhelmed with the information they need to feed into current systems for profile analysis, scenario preparation, and proposals. If they have to input data into this new lead system, it will impact the productivity of relationship managers. We'll need more staff and service desks in the branches to avoid longer queues. A potential increase in sales revenue that the lead system can bring would have to cover this additional operating cost.

On a flipchart sheet, Barbara was taking notes as people expressed themselves with some keywords that illustrated what was being said:

1. **Marketing**: Increase sales with information about opportunities.

2. **IT**: Avoid additional overtime costs to develop a new system.

3. **Operations**: Avoid overload of relationship managers feeding yet another system.

Barbara: Is there a solution that can make opportunity information available to Marketing without creating a new system?

Marketing Director: What do you mean?

Barbara: The operations manager said that branch staff already enter information into the systems for profile analysis, scenario preparation, and proposals. Could the lead information that is needed be extracted from these existing systems?

She drew a picture on the flipchart that summed up the idea in a simple way.

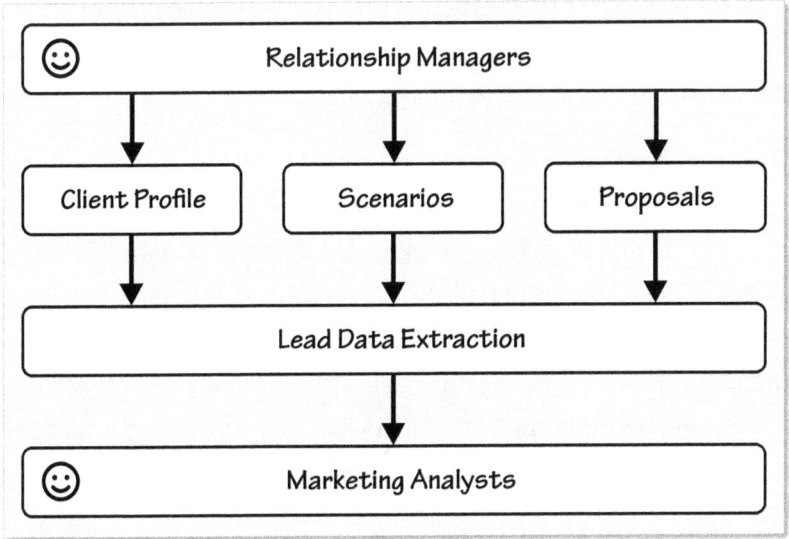

In this structure, it wouldn't be necessary to create a new system, only a search to access the data available in existing systems. The operations manager loved the idea because the branch wouldn't have any additional work and would continue to use the systems they were used to. The IT manager said this would be much simpler and easier to create and wouldn't depend on developers allocated to other systems. It could be produced quickly by the Business Intelligence team, who were experts in extracting data from existing databases. They just needed to ensure that all the data that Marketing wanted already existed in the original systems.

Barbara continued conducting the meeting and writing down the necessary lead information and where this information could be obtained, item by item, with everyone's collaboration. Now that everyone was involved in finding a solution to bring more value to the organization, the atmosphere of the meeting was completely different. They looked like members of the same team. I was captivated by how she guided the task and involved everyone in the design of a solution.

Some concessions had to be made because not all the information Marketing needed was available in those systems. However, adding a field to existing system screens is much simpler than introducing a new system. So she noted some minor improvements that would need to be implemented in the scenarios and proposals systems. These were negotiated with IT to be delivered later after the primary lead data were available and results could already be obtained.

> Marketing Director: I'm very satisfied with the design we have drawn up here to get the leads from proposals made at the branches. I believe it will work and be available within the timeframe. Can we also include the leads obtained at the Call Center for this project?

> Barbara: Does anyone here know if Call Center agents also use these systems?

There was general silence. Apparently, they hadn't invited anyone from the Call Center to the meeting, and I, who had that experience, was only there as a listener. I felt obliged to join in, but I didn't have the same experience level as the others, who knew everything about their fields. My heart raced, and I started sweating as I raised my trembling arm like a kid in a classroom. Barbara raised her eyebrows in surprise and, without a word, nodded for me to go on.

> Me: These systems are not available at the first Call Center service level.

When I spoke, everyone turned round to look at me, which was pretty uncomfortable. Their initial reaction was akin to, "Who the heck is this guy who wasn't even invited to the meeting?" But as I explained, the expressions changed to something I perceived as respect for a fellow team member.

> Me: Call Center agents need to direct customers interested in a specific service to the respective product departments. When physical documents need to be validated, they're directed to their local branch.

> Barbara: Thank you for the information. In that case, I suggest leaving the leads generated in the Call Center for a subsequent date and focusing now on those from the branch. Okay?

Everyone agreed, and the meeting ended with an action plan with well-defined completion dates and responsibilities. I admired Barbara's skill. She led the group gently and politely to create a collaborative environment and produced a solution that would meet everybody's expected outcomes.

I wondered if one day I could stand up there, leading a debate between areas with divergent goals and bringing them together as partners with a common goal. It seemed a far cry from someone who almost choked just speaking a few words at a meeting. I still had a lot to learn.

Chapter 10: Mindset

After the participants left, Barbara and I had the opportunity to introduce ourselves and chat. I said I was impressed with her ability to lead the workshop and design a solution that no one had thought of before.

> Barbara: Well, I wasn't the one who designed the solution. It was the group. I served as an auxiliary so everyone could speak and contribute their knowledge. I know little to nothing about marketing, sales, and systems, so I would never have come up with that solution on my own.

Her humility made her even more admirable to me. Oscar had said that humility is a virtue, and I could understand that better now. Without the ego of a know-it-all, Barbara was open to listening and accepting different points of view and could promote innovative solutions far beyond her knowledge. But how can you build that capability at scale and duplicate it across the organization?

Me: Oscar wants to change the bank's corporate culture. According to him, the default behavior of the people who work here is output-driven. We need to shift to outcome-driven behavior.

Barbara: What does corporate culture mean to you?

Now that was a difficult question! While I was trying to fathom the questions I already had, Barbara made me realize how much deeper the hole of my ignorance really was. I wanted to change something when I didn't even know what it was! I felt a little disconcerted, but I soon realized that this was Barbara's way of helping people. She asked questions far more than she gave answers, and that's how she helped people think and build a line of reasoning together.

Me: Well, when we talk about culture in general, I think of the culture of a people, a country, a region, or a community. Culture is what a group of people do as a recurring pattern. That includes typical festivals, music, cuisine, and how they live and relate to each other. In my family's culture, for example, my grandmother gathers all her children and grandchildren for dinner on Christmas Eve, and we say a prayer together. Then we eat like there's no tomorrow and collapse, full to bursting, onto the couch. It's always the same.

She smiled at my example and maybe related to it a little, too. Perhaps we didn't come from such different backgrounds.

Barbara: Okay then. You've defined culture in general. What's the difference between that and corporate culture?

Me: I think it's the same thing but in the context of a corporation or company. Is that right?

Barbara: It sounds about right to me. Culture is something that's effectively propagated through examples. If I were to spend Christmas at your house and wanted to integrate with your family, I wouldn't know the culture initially, so I would observe you before taking any initiative. When the food was on the table, I would probably notice that no one had served themselves before the prayer, and I would also wait for the appropriate time to serve myself. Little by little, I would adapt to how your family behaves at the table and to the issues discussed. It is learning by observing behavior. The same thing happens in a company.

I searched my memory to remember what my first few weeks at the bank had been like. At first, I didn't know how to behave, but I had, in fact, observed the behavior of others and tried to imitate them. The way we dress, the terms we use to serve the customer, the breaks with trips to the coffee corner, the constant complaining about everything, and even grumbling about the boss were standardized behaviors I had acquired from the corporate culture.

Me: So all behavior is learned by imitating the behavior of others?

Barbara: Well, that's not the whole story. We learn and share culture by repeating a collective behavior, but each person's behavior is individual and linked to their mindset.

Mindset—Oh great, here was another new word. These smart people, like Oscar and Barbara, just love these fancy words. I felt more than a tad skeptical, unenthusiastic, and, I'm sorry to say, lazy at the thought of learning another new concept. I had already learned the difference between output and outcome and now I would have to understand the difference between corporate culture and mindset. I took a deep breath and summoned up some courage:

Me: What do you mean by mindset?

Barbara: A person's behavior reflects what happens inside their mind. Mindset is the predisposition of each person to think, feel, and act the way they usually think, feel, and act.

Me: But isn't that just their behavior?

Barbara: Behavior is only the visible part of mindset—the part we can observe that affects other people and the environment. However, there is also an invisible part of mindset that involves each individual's beliefs, values, way of thinking, and emotional tendencies. This invisible part guides the visible behaviors.

Me: So it's not just imitation.

Barbara: Not at all. It's what we think and feel that shapes our actions. The decision to imitate the group's behavior happens first in the mind, based on a desire to be part of the group and a belief that learning the local culture is important to becoming part of it.

Barbara explained to me that what we say and do, our

reactions, gestures, and facial expressions—in fact, every action that is visibly observable by the people around us—begins in the internal space of the mind. In this invisible space are the beliefs, values, and mental models we use as filters to understand the world around us.

This intangible universe is formed dynamically and incrementally based on our individual experiences. That's why my mind differs from yours and anyone else's. We are unique.

Barbara also added that no two people have identical minds. Even identical twins, who share the same DNA, have different experiences right from their mother's womb and develop different ways of thinking, feeling, and acting. If you could take a complete photograph of my mind and compare it in a laboratory with another photograph from hours ago, they would not be identical because lived experiences continually modify us. No one is ever 100% done and finished. We are constantly transforming.

I understood that to change a person's behavior, you need to change the way they think and feel. The fact that I was there that day, talking to Barbara, and that I had accepted the offer to work in the Innovation Department represented a change in my behavior that was motivated by an internal change of thoughts and emotions that had motivated me to be there. Over the past few days, I had gone through several internal changes that had led me to turn my "indignation" into "action." That made sense.

In addition to my change of attitude in the Call Center, I had been inspired by how Julia dedicated herself to working with children at school, seeing in them the adults of the future. Now, I was encouraged to work in a more structured way when I saw Barbara conducting a meeting collaboratively to design an optimized solution within the bank.

But my change was individual. It didn't represent a change in corporate culture.

> Me: So what's the relationship between mindset and corporate culture?

> Barbara: When we observe a pattern of behaviors in a group of people motivated by beliefs and values common to all, we can say that it's a shared mindset. Corporate culture is the expression of a collective mindset.

Although each person has an individual and unique way of thinking, feeling, and acting, Barbara used the concept of a collective mindset, a collection of shared beliefs and values and standardized behaviors, to explain how corporate culture also has visible and invisible components.

> Me: If I understand correctly, to change the corporate culture we need to understand and transform the collective mindset we have today. Is that right?

> Barbara: It sounds like a good way to go. What do you think?

> Me: I think it makes sense, but I have no idea where to start.

> Barbara: Start by making a diagnosis.

Barbara suggested that I talk to people from different company departments to understand better how they think, feel, and act and identify patterns. She gave me some contacts and asked me to come back later to share what I had learned so we could plan the next steps.

To make the company innovative, we would need to change the collective mindset from output-driven to outcome-driven. The challenge made the hair on the back of my neck stand on end, but I began to believe that if my mindset was changing, then the mindset of others could change too.

Chapter 11: Interviews

The days following my first meeting with Barbara, the senior business analyst, were confusing but filled with learning. I talked to people from several departments, but at first, I didn't know what to do with the data from these interviews or what form the diagnosis of corporate culture should take. I took notes and wrote down things that seemed important to me in a notebook so that I could later review and structure my thoughts. This notebook is a fundamental source because I can clearly recall what I've learned. At the very least, I hope that clarity translates to this story.

If you've ever read *The Little Prince*, you might remember the hero's journey from the tiny planet Asteroid B612 to Earth. He visited several planets, met remarkable characters with whom he identified, accumulated learning, and began to understand the meaning of things. In some ways, the story of my interviews to diagnose the State Bank's corporate culture mirrored this little hero's adventures. Still, I want to clarify that they didn't happen chronologically in blocks, as they appear in the following chapters. The collection of information through interviews isn't sequential and structured, like climbing the rungs of a ladder: subject 1, subject 2, subject 3... Things happen more haphazardly, gathering pieces here and there, and the information collected fits into a puzzle that is assembled as the interviewer analyzes the data. What you will read in the following chapters was compiled after this analysis.

I would also like to emphasize that while conducting interviews is a valuable technique for understanding an organization, it requires some care. I was lucky to be mentored by Barbara and would like to share some tips that helped me talk to people. These tips may make a difference if you need to gather information through interviews.

1. Don't act like an inspector.

The interview is a moment of intimate conversation in which the interviewee can confide information they might not otherwise disclose. However, they will only do that if they don't feel threatened by you or the outcome of the interview. If the interviewee feels, in any way, that they're being evaluated or judged, they will assume a defensive posture and will tend to say what they think you want to hear. It's similar to a job interview where the candidate wants to make a good impression or a police investigation when the officer cautions a suspect: "Anything you say can and will be used against you."

When interviewing people, I always made it clear that the purpose was not to evaluate my interviewees but rather the corporate culture itself—how the company is organized and its processes, systems, and rules. Whenever I noticed an interviewee was uncomfortable answering some questions, I put myself in their place and realized they might feel threatened. I clarified that I wasn't there to reprimand anyone—I don't even have that authority. My goal was to improve the work environment, and I needed their help.

I learned that sharing the purpose of my work with the interviewee makes them a partner in the organizational transformation I'm pursuing. Although the interview is essentially an investigative technique, make it collaborative to create alliances and draw people into the outcomes you seek to generate.

2. Don't make assumptions.

In one of the interviews, I arrived asking questions about corporate culture, outputs, and outcomes, and it took a while to realize that my interviewee had no idea what these terms mean or even that the bank has an Innovation Department.

In another, I went to see what I thought was a working system only to find that it had never existed—development had been canceled before it began. It wasn't exactly the information I had anticipated, but it was worth its weight in gold at the time.

It's essential to prepare for an interview beforehand with questions you intend to ask or even some hypotheses you would like to validate with the interviewees. However, you should be open to receiving information contrary to your expectations. Your hypotheses may be misguided, and the interviewees may open your eyes to a world of other possibilities that require you to deviate from the questions you had previously prepared. Take advantage of opportunities to explore uncharted waters.

To find a gold nugget, you may need to dig deeper than you bargained for. If you end up finding a diamond, even better.

3. Develop rapport with the interviewee.

Rapport is a relationship of mutual trust and emotional affinity. Sometimes, it develops naturally and effortlessly. This resonance was immediate with some of the people I interviewed, and the conversation flowed easily. It's easy to talk about life and confide in someone you feel comfortable with, even on personal or sensitive matters.

But that doesn't happen with everyone. I confess that I felt a particular dislike for some people. I know this isn't a positive point, but surely you also have acquaintances you don't feel comfortable with. The conversation usually doesn't flow, and the few times it does, it's about as pleasant as doing income tax returns. I felt these types either weren't interested in me or that nothing I could do or say would be relevant to them. Those were the most difficult interviews.

A sympathetic, rather than unsympathetic, relationship between interviewer and interviewee is essential to the success of an interview. Therefore, the interviewer cannot rely on luck to find people they naturally identify with. In an interview, the interviewer is responsible for building this relationship using rapport development techniques.

People tend to identify with and trust other people with similar characteristics. So I sought common ground with my interviewees, identifying shared narratives, tastes, experiences, and opinions to build a climate of affinity.

I did this by avoiding getting straight down to business. Instead, I began the interview with personal questions unrelated to the purpose of the interview, which helped identify mutual interests and break the ice.

Where do you live?

What team do you support?

Do you have children?

Do you play any sports?

Where did you go on vacation?

I would contribute openly to the conversation, drawing attention to what we had in common and the basis for mutual trust. Investing a few minutes in building this rapport made the atmosphere more pleasant and the interviews more productive.

A word of caution: I must make one thing very clear regarding this technique for establishing rapport. I'm not advising anyone to invent an aging aunt in a rural town or fake being a lifelong fan of a different team to seem similar to their interviewee. Deceit does not build trust. It might work as a form of manipulation for a short period, but once discovered, it destroys the deceiver's relationships and reputation.

Establishing rapport is based on the premise that we have genuine similarities with someone. We need to identify and focus on them honestly to build the relationship. That's why the typical subject of elevator talk is the weather.

Turned out hot today, didn't it?

In the elevator, there's awkward silence in a cramped environment from which we cannot escape, so we're obliged to interact with people we don't even know.

Yes, but the forecast says it'll cool down tomorrow.

Weather is something you have in common with anyone.

Chapter 12: Cow Trail

One of my first interviews was with the operations manager who attended the workshop with Barbara. He was elated when they decided not to create a new system and that the branch employees would continue to use the existing ones. This caught my attention because I know that the systems used in the branches are already quite outdated. I had thought an innovation might be well received here.

> Me: Did you consider that developing a new system could be an opportunity to improve the branch environment?

> Operations Manager: Heaven preserve us from a change of system! If it ain't broke, don't fix it. Our team is well-trained and knows how to use the systems we have. A change would force us to retrain everyone. And new systems always come with new problems. It's better to live with the problems we're used to and know how to get around than to start all over again.

I remained unconvinced that the system wasn't broken. And,

even if it weren't, as Oscar had already warned me, fintech companies were gaining space in our market with each passing day. The forecast was that the competition would soon overtake the State Bank. This made the aversion to a new system in the branches arouse my curiosity even more.

I wanted to understand this resistance better from the point of view of those on the front line serving customers. So I spoke to Cesar. Remember him? My soccer friend who was also my account manager.

> Cesar: Everyone loves to complain about how things are, the processes, the systems, the infrastructure— everything. But when it comes to change, people don't support it and even seem to sabotage any kind of change. I mean, look at it closely! No one really wants to change anything. Even those who complain the most seem to like complaining. If you solve the problem, what will they complain about?

I felt particularly ashamed because I could relate to the profile he was describing. I thought about the many times I'd complained about something and put myself in a position of zero responsibility. As if solving the problem was beyond me. For example, the daily complaints I made about the heat in my apartment. It's not as if an air conditioner would spontaneously sprout from fungus cultivated in the heat and humidity of my room. If I wanted to change my situation, I couldn't just complain—I had to do something about it. But that was a personal case. I was there to change the corporate culture.

> Me: Could you give me an example of resistance to

change at the branch?

Cesar went on to tell me of some attempts at change that were unsuccessful. In one of them, a new system was implemented to replace one of the main systems used by the branch staff. The old system had a text and command interface that you had to memorize and write on a command line, typical of systems from the 1970s. They created a new system with a graphic interface, buttons, and navigation windows that would be more intuitive and easier for new employees to learn. But the system didn't take off. The former employees refused to use it and claimed that the old system was faster and better suited to their needs.

I was shocked that somebody would prefer to stick with something outdated and not trade it in for something more modern. It's like offering someone an iPhone and finding out they prefer their old Nokia, which is about as handy as a brick.

> Cesar: If you don't believe me, here's how we still check foreign exchange operations.

Cesar opened his terminal and showed a screen with text commands that remained the primary way account managers in the branches handled some of the information.

> Me: Is it the same system as in the 70s?

> Cesar: We're so used to it that it's hard to change.

Changing the way you think takes a lot of energy! The human brain organizes itself through neural connections that create pathways through which we repeat the way we think and act in patterns of behavior.

Cesar: It's like a cow trail!

Me: A cow trail?

Cesar: Yeah. Have you never seen one? My uncle used to raise cattle in the countryside, and my cousins and I would spend our holidays on his farm. We loved to be at one with nature and explore the beautiful waterfalls and landscapes in the area. But walking through the undergrowth is hard—you have to cut your way with a machete. So we always found the paths the cows used, one behind the other in single file. The paths are worn into the ground and become actual trails where it's much easier to make your way. We would always follow these "cow trails" until we found a stream.

I didn't know until then that Cesar had spent his childhood in the countryside. But his metaphor made sense and, to some degree, represents the pathways the mind develops over time and through which behavior patterns are established. In the case of the "cow trail," this behavior represents not only an individual pattern but a collective one. The cows follow each other along these trails and reinforce the marks on the ground, making it easier and easier to follow, just like the repeated behavior that creates a corporate culture. A cow that wants to try a different path will have a much harder time exploring it, so it ends up following the other cows down the standard path. What a great metaphor!

Cesar: If you think about it, resistance to change is a successful energy-saving strategy.

Saving energy seems to be the standard functioning of the

human brain and how our corporate mindset today has been structured. New ideas are quickly discredited and discarded because change takes energy to implement. It seems easier to maintain the status quo.

In a conversation with Rodrigo about my challenge to make the company more innovative, he drew my attention to an unwritten directive that I had already heard in the hallways and that, although it was said by people with a mocking tone, reflected accurately the corporate culture of our company:

> Rodrigo: We follow the unwritten rule: "Any initiative will be severely punished!"
>
> Me: Come on, Rodrigo! I know people say this in the cafe, but do you really believe it?
>
> Rodrigo: I'm fully convinced that it's 100% true. I once made the mistake of coming up with an idea that could improve our work.
>
> Me: And what happened?
>
> Rodrigo: My boss told me to research the subject more and prepare a feasibility study. I spent ages creating a presentation that was then butchered by everyone and shelved. I did a motherload of extra work for nothing. After that, I learned to follow procedures and ask no questions.

I felt sorry for Rodrigo. He tried to stray from the cow trail to find something better but couldn't convince others and wasn't even commended for his effort. He went on to develop a metaphor related to food, his favorite subject, which I found curious because it didn't at all represent his true behavior in the kitchen:

> Rodrigo: The way we work here at the bank is like making food in a restaurant. You have to follow the recipe without question. The recipe says 250 grams of flour, I add 250 grams of flour. No more, no less. If it doesn't turn out well, it's not my fault. It's the recipe!

> Me: What if the recipe is wrong?

> Rodrigo: It's the problem of whoever wrote the recipe. Not mine.

> Me: Rodrigo, I know you love cooking. At home, do you always follow the recipe without changing anything?

> Rodrigo: Well, at home, it's different. I use the recipe as the starting point and not the endpoint. When I cook, I always tweak the recipe to make it tastier. In fact, I often end up creating a new recipe by adding something I have in the fridge.

> Me: Why would working at home be different from working in a restaurant?

> Rodrigo: Because, at home, I'm not forced to make the food. I make food for pleasure. It's not work, it's fun.

I remembered a phrase I had read in Mark Twain's *The Adventures of Tom Sawyer* and have never forgotten: "Work consists of whatever a body is obliged to do. Play consists of whatever a body is not obliged to do."

This seems to be a reasonably typical distinction that affects behavior. In an output-driven mindset, the commitment is to get the job done. People who act in this way tend to behave rigidly. They're resistant to change and more likely to reject new ideas.

When Rodrigo makes food at home, he's committed to the outcome and only follows the recipe if he believes it's the best way to achieve the desired result. If, during the preparation, the mixture doesn't bind or the sauce doesn't thicken, he will immediately go off the cow trail and find an alternative way to get the best result. It doesn't matter if the change consumes energy, creativity, and risk. He won't accept something that doesn't taste good. Blaming the recipe for failure is not an option.

Another thing that caught my attention is that when he's cooking at home, Rodrigo often changes the recipe even though there's nothing wrong with it. He does things differently because he wants to make something even tastier, like when he created the mushroom omelet with scallions. He creates new recipes to explore ideas and achieve better outcomes. I wrote down the respective behaviors of the output- and outcome-driven mindsets:

Output-Driven Mindset
- **Rigid:** I resist change and avoid new ideas.

Outcome-Driven Mindset
- **Adaptable:** I challenge the status quo.

Just one last personal account before concluding this chapter. I accepted Cesar's offer and took out a payroll loan to buy an air conditioner for my room. The interest rates for employees are attractive and I was able to pay in 12 installments without compromising my budget.

It's no use just complaining about life. I needed to turn my indignation into action.

Chapter 13: Rule of Three

I figured that, from customer complaints, I could identify likely corporate culture issues and possibly identify some good opportunities for innovation. With that in mind, I gathered as much information as I could.

In an interview with a credit analyst, I asked what the main customer complaints were. In that conversation, I was struck by an interesting situation involving a restrictive rule related to assets used for loan collateral.

> Credit Analyst: Sometimes we miss business opportunities because the customer doesn't meet the Rule of Three when registering collateral.

Didn't understand what he meant? Neither did I at first. Let's break it down:

Collateral is an asset or equity that a debtor agrees to give to the bank if he can't repay a loan. It can be real estate, jewelry, vehicles, works of art—anything of value that he owns.

The Rule of Three is the basic technique we learn in school to find an unknown number in a pair of equivalent fractions when we know the three other numbers. At least, that was the Rule of Three I had learned.

> Credit Analyst: No! This Rule of Three has nothing to do with school. The Rule of Three in loans, which is known to everyone here in the area, is as follows: "A loan cannot be granted with more than three assets as collateral."

> Me: If I understand correctly, this rule imposes a restriction. For example, if a customer wants to offer five assets as collateral, the loan can't be approved.

> Credit Analyst: Kind of. But although they can't take out one loan, they can take out two. So, to get around this, we divide the loan into two loan agreements, one with three collateral assets and the other with two. It almost always works out.

He explained that this "almost always" situation sometimes doesn't work out, which is where complaints arise and customers are lost. Customers are dissatisfied and take their business to another institution. Dividing the loan into smaller slices is a "hack" (or workaround) that the loan team uses to circumvent the Rule of Three. However, besides making the loan more complex, this solution has limitations. I'll give you an example with simple dummy numbers that will make the situation easy to understand.

Imagine that a customer wants to take out a loan and needs to provide collateral for 1,000 currency units. The specific currency is irrelevant in this case. Follow the reasoning. The customer has five collateral assets worth 200 each. Due to the restriction imposed by the Rule of Three, he cannot make a single loan agreement and must divide it into two loans using three collateral assets in the first and two in the second. A loan of 600 and a loan of 400 would be ideal. The problem is that loans under 500 are classified under other legislation that doesn't apply to that customer's conditions. He can't make two loans of 500 because he can't split one of the collateral assets and put half in each loan. As a result, one loan has a surplus of collateral, and the other lacks it.

> Credit Analyst: We're attempting to modify the system to enable this type of transaction by dividing a fraction of collateral for each loan.

> Me: What a pain! What's the reason for this Rule of Three?

> Credit Analyst: Uh... why does it exist? What do you mean?!

He looked at me in astonishment, as if I had asked the most outlandish question. It was like asking a religious person about the origin of God: *God has no origin. He simply is. He is beyond the beginning of time. He is the origin of everything!*

Business rules can't be a dogma of faith. They're created from reason in a conscious and structured way to avoid risks or exploit opportunities. There's no rule without justification (or there shouldn't be). I'll give you an example to illustrate:

Rule 1 — An incapacitated person may not open a checking account.

This is a rule that sets a constraint. It was created to avoid customers failing to comply with their obligations, leaving the bank without legal recourse to demand compliance. It's not possible to prosecute an incapacitated person because they're not responsible for their actions.

Other rules define how to tell if a person has mental capacity.

Rule 2 – Persons deemed incapable of personally performing the acts of civil life:

A. children under 16 years of age,

B. persons who, due to illness or mental deficiency, do not have the necessary discernment to practice these acts, or,

C. persons who cannot express their will, even for a transitory reason.

Note: While unconscious in the hospital, Oscar's mother came under Rule 2C, allowing us to register the power of attorney that gave Oscar access to his account.

The point I want to make here is that rules always have a logical origin and aren't unquestionable dogmas. More important than obeying the rule is ensuring that its objectives, i.e., the risks it supposedly avoids or the opportunities it claims to nurture, are being fulfilled. In other words, committing to a rule's expected outcome is necessary.

> Credit Analyst: I have no idea why this Rule of Three was created. It's probably some legal restriction. It's better to check that with the Legal people.

I questioned several people from the Legal Department, and none of them could inform me of any legal restrictions that would limit the number of assets used as collateral in a loan. I even considered that it could mitigate risks, but a risk analyst told me that the effect was the opposite.

> Risk Analyst: From a risk point of view, the lower the number of collateral assets, the riskier the loan is. A greater number of collateral assets dilutes the risk that one of them cannot be liquidated in the event of non-payment of the debt.

So, I discarded this hypothesis and went looking for the origin of the Rule of Three elsewhere. As no one in the Credit or Legal area knew the reason for this rule, I decided to talk to the IT people who developed the credit system and implemented the restriction.

> Systems Analyst: This rule is ancient. It already existed when I started working here. If the Credit people don't know the source, I can try to reverse engineer the source code to see if I can figure anything out.

Reverse engineering is a technique in which one reads the computer program that automates a process in an attempt to understand its logic. It's called "reverse" because it is in the opposite direction to the creation of a program. Usually, someone specifies a business process and its rules; from this specification, the computer programs that automate the process are created. However, when the origin is no longer known, an investigation starting from the code may be informative.

I felt like an archaeologist trying to unravel the customs of the lost civilization of Atlantis from excavations and artifacts. I would never have been able to do this without the help of the systems analyst. In addition to restricted access to these codes, this technique requires a knowledge of programming languages I didn't have.

> Systems Analyst: I figured out the origin of the Rule of Three. Basically, it isn't a business rule. It's a restriction prompted by a decades-old implementation flaw in the loan system that no one has ever fixed.

I'm not tech-savvy, but I'll explain what happened the way he explained it to me. I hope it's clear.

The system must store information about the amount, customer, start date, number of installments, and collateral assets for each loan in a database. The loan database is structured as a table, with each row representing a loan.

Value	Customer	Start	Installments	Collateral Asset 1	Collateral Asset 2	Collateral Asset 3
500	Paul	28/12/23	12	House	Car	Jewelry
500	Paul	28/12/23	12	Watch	Painting	—
1000	Ann	06/01/24	36	Lot		

Obviously, my example is simplified, but you can see that this structure makes it impossible to put more than three collateral assets on the same loan. The systems analyst told me the collateral should have been recorded in a separate table, making it possible to include as many collateral assets as needed for each loan. The professional who created the system was likely inexperienced or under too much pressure and used this structure. Time passed, and people in the lending area thought the business had imposed the rule. It hadn't. The Rule of Three was a limitation imposed by a poorly designed system.

Later, I saw that this wasn't a particularly unusual situation. Someone creates an improvised solution to a problem, and it ends up becoming permanent, enforcing a series of limitations that no one comes back to review and correct. Over time, the "cow trail" becomes established, and people get so accustomed to the rule that they don't question it and can no longer see beyond it.

It doesn't mean they're not uncomfortable. Note that the credit area is considering making a new system for fractioning collateral, which would be a much more complex solution than allowing you to add more than three collateral assets to the same loan.

I reflected that the output-driven mindset leads to situations where following rules is unquestionable. If people were focused on the outcome, they would question the regulations to identify their justification and ensure the result they expected.

I noted one more difference in behavior in my notebook.

Output-Driven Mindset

- **Obedient:** I follow explicit instructions without question.

Outcome-Driven Mindset

- **Creative:** I figure out how to achieve the best result.

After this analysis, the systems analyst told me that he was going to request the cancellation of the project that created the fractional collateral and start a project to eliminate the restriction of the infamous Rule of Three to allow an unlimited number of collateral assets per loan.

> Systems Analyst: This change will be simpler, cheaper, and can be implemented in a shorter timeframe.

> Me: And you won't have to divide a loan into several more minor contracts when there is multiple-asset collateral. It will be simpler for everyone.

> Systems Analyst: Yes. It's an excellent change. Thank you for helping us identify it.

I reflected on my actions, trying to identify situations where I obey rules without question. Why can't I just call the pretty lady on the sixth floor? Why do I believe I don't stand a chance with her? It's not written anywhere. It's just a restriction that I have imposed on myself. I started thinking of a creative way to get closer to Julia. Just like the rules of the loan system, perhaps the rules of the game of love are also ready to be rewritten.

Chapter 14: To the Rhythm of the Orchestra

When I was a boy, I was in the school band. I never had much musical talent and always underrated my contribution. While some of my classmates played wind instruments or strings with various sounds and a complex score, I played the floor tom—that large, cylindrical drum that hardly varies throughout the entire song: *Tum, tum. Tum, tum. Tum, tum...*

The band conductor, however, always told me that my part was the most important because I guided the rhythm of all the other instruments by setting the rhythm for the band to play in harmony. The *tum, tum* made by the floor tom is like the beating of a heart, he said, to encourage me. That morning, my heart was setting the rhythm for a full-bodied serenade to Julia.

If I had to choose a theme song for our relationship, I'd choose The Carpenters' cover of "Please Mr. Postman."

Please Mister Postman, look and see.
(Oh, yeah) Is there a letter in your bag for me?

Listening to this fragment on the radio, I had an idea of how I could approach the beautiful girl from the sixth floor. I'll tell you that story at the end of this chapter. But first, I want to tell you the results of some other interviews that led me to look back on my history as a member of the school band.

One of the names on the list of nominations for my interviews was Mello, the marketing director. The same one who had participated in the workshop with Barbara and who was interested in the lead information to create sales campaigns for customers.

Mello was elegant, friendly, and what you might call "energetic." He had a way of speaking that emanated energy and optimism. He was like a politician who was always on the campaign trail. And I have to say that if he were a politician, it would be difficult not to vote for him, such is the charisma and assertiveness with which he always expressed his arguments.

> Mello: I'm glad you're working with Oscar in the Innovation Department. Innovation has always made a difference here at the State Bank and will keep us as market leaders. Did you know that we were the first bank to implement a customer self-service system and one of the first to provide services over the Internet?

He always liked to present the company as the embodiment of virtue, but I knew it was somewhat misleading. The innovations he mentioned, such as self-service and the Internet, are real cases, but they were from the last century. The situation was now quite different, with a much more competitive market of small businesses offering differentiated services and leaving the State Bank eating dust.

Me: How do you evaluate innovation today in our company?

Mello: We're soaring! Some people think that the State Bank is outdated, but that's a misconception that we'll soon be changing. I don't know if you're aware, but we're launching a campaign this year to announce the new customer service model using extended intelligence—something that will revolutionize the market and delight our customers.

Me: Extended intelligence? What's that?

Mello: Top-notch innovation, created here at the bank by the Operations staff. It uses the best artificial intelligence with the best human intelligence in a single service platform.

Me: Interesting! How does it work?

Mello: The old service systems are outdated. When customers get in touch through a service channel, they want to be served by a person, not a robot. They want to chat, place their orders, and clarify their doubts by talking naturally, not having to listen to a menu of options, and then type 1, 2, or 3. But they also don't want to wait in line for a long time until an agent is available. They want to be answered at the first ring and explain what they need immediately. Extended intelligence can interact in natural language with multiple customers while also interacting with various experts who monitor calls and resolve more complex issues in real time. It's a mixture that takes advantage of technology, enhancing the productivity of our team of super-experienced professionals. It's revolutionary!

It was impossible not to be infected by Mello's excitement. According to him, this innovation would uphold the State Bank's ground-breaking tradition and potentially alter market perception.

Mello: But the quality of service alone won't guarantee the value of our brand. Do you know that the duck egg is larger and more nutritious than the chicken egg? Yet the sale of chicken eggs is much higher. Do you know why? Because when she lays an egg, the hen starts clucking like there's no tomorrow!

Me: Are you talking about advertising?

Mello: I sure am! Without proper advertising, there's no point in getting this technology on the air. We're working on a historic campaign. Our brand will be on TV, radio, the Internet, and billboards everywhere. We're hiring screenwriters, TV and cinema stars, and digital influencers. Like self-service and the Internet, extended intelligence is a trend that will be everywhere before long. When you think of EI, you will associate it with the State Bank because it was the first to innovate.

It was all very exciting, and it had been a while since the bank's name had been associated with innovation. But all that investment didn't match the austere cost-containment policy

I saw in other areas.

> Me: Isn't the bank cutting costs? Do you have the funding for this super campaign?

> Mello: I already have the budget secured. You're right to point out that the bank is cutting costs, and our goal earlier this year was also to reduce marketing costs. But I showed the Budget Committee that saving on brand awareness was short-sighted. It's time to invest heavily in advertising and take advantage of this innovation. We cannot be left behind.

If Mello had managed to increase the budget in his area, there would probably have been cuts in other places, and I was curious to know where the money had come from. I spoke with one of the advisors who serves as a member of the Budget Committee.

> Advisor: Our budget is distributed annually among the departments, but we make quarterly reviews to accommodate necessary changes according to the macroeconomic scenario or because of an opportunity.

> Me: In the last review, I heard that Marketing got a hefty sum to implement an advertising campaign.

> Advisor: Yes. They presented a robust study to defend an investment well above the initial forecast. We talked to HR and Operations reps, who agreed to reduce their budgets. The Committee serves precisely to arbitrate on these issues.

To unravel the mystery, I gathered information from these

places as well. I knew that HR had already heavily reduced training budgets in recent years, and I was curious about how they would go about reducing them further.

HR Director: Since the pandemic, we've conducted almost all of our training through online video courses. We signed an agreement with a platform, and our employees can access these courses from home, in their own time, and at their own pace. The cost is much lower than face-to-face training, and we no longer need to spend on a room, equipment, coffee break, or instructor. Now, that's innovation! You can ask Oscar.

Me: What about the results of the training? Is it effective?

HR Director: We've had excellent evaluations of the courses. Employees love to do training from home.

Me: But what about the learning outcome? After training, are employees performing well in the role they were trained for?

HR Director: Well, we can't measure that. Performance assessment should be done by their departments. It's not up to HR.

Of course, the employees love doing the training at home! Everyone wants to stay home, especially watching a nice little video while eating popcorn on the sofa. I have nothing against it, but the lack of performance measurement related to the training results set off alarm bells. How could you tell if the training was working?

Anyway, the question that led me to this interview was how

they had managed to reduce the HR budget in the last quarter. These online courses had been in place for much longer, so the new cost reduction had to come from another source.

HR Director: We reduced the costs of oversized salaries. Over the years, some very old employees had accumulated raises and benefits and had salaries far above the payroll average. We created a voluntary redundancy program to lighten the payroll and secured several employees' adhesion in this profile.

I immediately remembered my conversation with Oscar the day he offered me a job in the Innovation Department. He had told me that the bank was losing "talent" because more experienced employees were leaving to work at companies that offered more attractive conditions. What he didn't tell me, and probably didn't know either, is that HR was encouraging this outflow of talent with a voluntary redundancy program.

The information I got from HR left me a little stunned, but it doesn't begin to compare to what I learned from interviewing the operations director.

Operations Director: I don't think I'll be able to talk to you right now. I'm swamped here, and there's an emergency that I need to resolve today.

Me: I'm sorry. I don't want to take up too much of your time, but we've already rescheduled this interview twice. If you could just give me five minutes, it would benefit the study the Innovation Department is conducting.

Operations Director: Oscar told me about it. I'll give

you five minutes, but that's all. I have a lot to do today, and there's no one to help me. I just don't have a life anymore. There was a time when I had an elite team around here. I could delegate tasks, and I knew everything would be done. But today, my senior team has abandoned me, and I'm surrounded by juniors who don't have a clue what needs to be done. I have to have a hand in everything. I'm constantly solving problems that aren't the director's job, but if I don't, it's game over.

And that's how it was. He opened up about how overworked he was, which indicated that the HR policy was wreaking havoc on the Operations Department. The most experienced employees were no longer available, and the new employees weren't receiving the necessary training to fulfill their roles properly.

I still had my question about the budget reduction. If the reduction in the payroll had been attributed to the HR budget, the reduction in the Operations budget must have come from some investment that was initially planned and then canceled in the quarterly review.

Me: I heard they had to reduce the budget planned for this quarter so that the bank could reallocate funds to Marketing.

Operations Director: Yes. We canceled a project that wasn't going to work out anyway. In the end, it was a sound decision. It would have been a waste of money, and we wouldn't have had time to develop it.

Me: Would you mind telling me which project it was?

Operations Director: We wanted to develop a new service platform using artificial intelligence to relieve the Operations team and leverage the expertise of our best specialists.

Me: Was the project, by any chance, called extended intelligence?

Operations Director: Yes, it was. Have you heard of it?

Me: Yes. Was it canceled?

Operations Director: Yeah, but it's for the best. I don't think it was plausible. The technology needed to implement it is still very new, and we don't entirely understand how it works. Even if we had total mastery of the technology, we no longer have the specialists to assemble the back-office team to monitor the services and support their operation.

Me: Because the senior staff has left, and the junior team doesn't have the necessary training.

Operations Director: Exactly. At least we could free up the money for the Marketing people to do something useful. They seem to be on to a good thing. I'm not sure what it is, but they're confident the investment will bring a good return.

He didn't know what it was, but I did, and I had to tell him the uncomfortable and embarrassing truth. What Marketing was doing was a million-dollar campaign for a project that had been canceled. The most ridiculous thing is that the project had been canceled to free up the money that would be used to finance the campaign to promote it. It was a hungry dragon eating its own tail.

I was beginning to grasp the scenario Oscar had told me about, which concerned the survival of the business. But it wasn't just the threat of competition that put the bank at risk. The bank was at risk because of its inability to perceive what was happening and align its activities.

That's what reminded me of the school band. In one of the rehearsals, where nothing seemed to be going right, our conductor taught us a valuable lesson.

> Conductor: A band can only work if everyone plays in harmony. Even the most talented musicians will produce nothing of value if they play out of tune with each other. The result is this racket you're making. We need to listen to each other.

He asked me to set the rhythm with the floor tom. Then he introduced each instrument, one at a time, making sure we could hear each other and keep the rhythm. The result was a sweet-toned melody we had never produced before. We were all delighted and proud.

Focusing on outcome pushes us beyond the limits of our perspective and forces us to seek collaboration with others. I jotted down a summary of what I had learned about different types of behavior.

Output-Driven Mindset

- **Individualistic:** I ignore other points of view.

Outcome-Driven Mindset

- **Collaborative:** I take responsibility for collaboration and shared understanding.

On my way home, I talked to the doorman of the building, who told me that although Julia had asked every day, her package had not yet arrived. I knew Rodrigo had experience buying kitchen utensils on the Chinese website that Julia had used. I asked him if delays were common, and he told me that sometimes purchases are retained at the post office, waiting for the buyer to pick them up and pay an additional import fee. I searched the website and found out how to track the purchase. I called apartment 604 late in the afternoon, and Julia answered.

Me: Maybe your package has been retained at the post office?

Julia: What do you mean?

Me: Aren't you waiting for the delivery of an order from a Chinese website?

Julia: Yes!

Me: I was thinking about it, and I remembered that these parcels sometimes get retained at the post office because they need an additional import fee payment. Have you checked that?

Julia: No, I haven't. I don't even know how to.

Me: I have the post office website open on my computer. Would you like to take a look using your purchase details? We can check it together.

Julia: 805. Are you sure it won't be any bother?

Me: Not at all!

She recognized my voice and remembered my apartment number. That's got to mean something! I have snacks and cold drinks in the fridge. And you know what song is playing on the radio?

Please Mister Postman, look and see.
(Oh, yeah) Is there a letter in your bag for me?

Chapter 15: Magic

Julia arrived at my apartment a few minutes later. She was wearing a baggy T-shirt, shorts, and flip-flops—a cozy outfit for relaxing at home. She took the elevator and came upstairs without ceremony. "I'm glad she feels at home," I thought. I couldn't help wondering if a touch of lipstick would be a promising sign, but she was makeup-free—not that she needed any. She was beautiful, as God created her.

I invited her in to check the post office website together and find out what could have happened to her parcel.

> Me: It's so hot today, isn't it? I've heard this is the hottest it's been in the last 30 years.

> Julia: Yes, it really is!

An awkward silence filled the room.

> Me: Would you like a cold drink?

> Julia: A glass of cold water would be great. Thanks.

As I got her the water, I tried to extend the weather theme.

> Me: Luckily, I've just had an air-con installed in my bedroom.

> Julia: In the bedroom?

She looked at the bedroom door and a second of silence followed that seemed like an excruciating eternity. What had she understood from the information I had shared so innocently? That I intended to take her to the bedroom on the first date? Which, by the way, wasn't even a date? She had just come to solve a problem with a delivery. What difference would my air conditioning make for her?

A bead of sweat appeared on my forehead as I attempted to make the atmosphere less tense.

> Me: If I close the living room windows and open the bedroom door, the whole apartment will be cooler. I'll just get my laptop. Let's see if we can find your package.

Oh my God, I felt so insecure! If only there were a manual for these situations. Why don't they teach us at school how to deal with the person we're interested in? What good are physics, chemistry, and mathematics at a time like this? I know that, by gravity, two bodies attract each other, that oxytocin is a hormone that helps to establish social bonds of affection, and that 1+1=2. But I don't seem to know how to apply any of that at life's critical moments!

It would be better to focus on what Julia needed and get over these feelings as quickly as possible. I put the laptop on the living room table, and she sat beside me. We visited the website where she had made the purchases and checked the post office site, confirming that her package was being held at the central post office, awaiting payment of import and collection fees. She would have to go there personally to pick it up.

Me: May I ask what you bought?

Julia: You may, but don't judge me! It's a magic kit.

Me: With tricks, like the ones they do in the circus? A scarf that disappears, a knife that doesn't cut, a coin that comes out from behind the ear...

Julia: Exactly. I want to learn some magic tricks for the kids at school. I think they'll like it.

Me: I love magic! I know a few tricks I can teach you. Let me get a deck of cards to show you.

And, just like magic, my discomfort disappeared. We spent hours talking, watching videos on the Internet, sharing magic tricks, telling stories, and laughing. One common interest opened the door to several others.

I felt so comfortable that I told her about my experiences at work: my change of role from the Call Center to the Innovation Department, the transformation challenge that Oscar wanted to implement in the company, how I had learned from different interviews, the problems I had already identified, and all the opportunities for improvement that could be explored. As I spoke, I noticed that Julia was in awe of everything I was experiencing and, at the same time, a feeling that I was not used to—pride. The satisfaction of work that was meaningful. It was the same thing as when we met, and I was delighted with the way Julia talked about her work. Except now, I was the one talking.

I arranged to pick up her package with her—it was close to where I worked. That night, we formed a special bond of friendship and understanding, making it clear to me that we were no longer just neighbors. We had much to explore.

As she said goodbye, I wanted to kiss her, but I wasn't brave enough. She kissed me on the cheek and thanked me. "See you soon," she said.

And I slept like an enchanted baby in the arms of a fairy, my magical dreams at the perfect temperature. With the air conditioning on.

Chapter 16: New Routine

My mornings became much more pleasurable. Waking up for work no longer felt like a cruel punishment. I woke up excited, like someone about to watch the next episode of their favorite TV series. I couldn't wait to find out what the day would bring.

I was waking up earlier than before, so I had time to eat a good breakfast. In addition to the bread and butter on the griddle, I had already tried yogurt, granola, fruit, and cheese on toast. But my favorite was scrambled eggs, now the most frequent choice on my new morning menu.

One day, I tried going to work by bus instead of the subway to see if it was better. It wasn't. It took twice as long. "That's okay," I thought. "It was an experiment to validate a hypothesis." I began to try new things frequently. Most were epic failures. Still, I put them down to learning. Each was another lived experience, another chance to discover something new by letting life take me.

Speaking of which, I never saw the lady with the toy guitar again. I confess that I was worried about her. As if by some mystical force, I felt responsible. My life had begun to change a lot from that day on. Had her life changed, too? For better or for worse? What had happened? What was the power of Dona Rosa's charm? I ended up asking some colleagues at the bank about her. Most didn't know who I was talking about, but one colleague seemed to remember.

> Colleague: That old lady who always sings the same song out of tune with a toy guitar?

> Me: Yes, that's her.

> Colleague: I think she moved to another spot. I saw her two stations after Central. Probably pays better there.

I felt better knowing that she wasn't a figment of my imagination, that she existed and was still around. Nothing to get superstitious about.

That day, I arrived at the bank, swiped my card, clocked in, and headed straight to Oscar's room for a meeting we had scheduled first thing. Oscar was at his desk fiddling with his computer and motioned for me to sit down while he finished writing. He was always working on something. As soon as he was done, he spoke.

> Oscar: We had a board meeting yesterday, and your name was mentioned more than once.

I froze. While I had been enjoying myself, asking questions and discovering acutely embarrassing mistakes, I hadn't even considered that many of the people I had talked to were directors of the bank (the Hollywood stars, remember?) and that I might be exposing these people to their peers. It looked as though my days at the Innovation Department were numbered.

Me: I hope I didn't upset anyone.

Oscar: Quite the opposite! I heard great things about you.

Me: Really?!

Oscar: Well, the operations director was complaining that he didn't have time to talk to you, but I insisted that he make some. Then things turned out rather well, didn't they?

Me: Well, it was pretty quick, but I found out some important things that I included in a report that I was going to present to you today.

Even though no one had read my report, the directors had been able to put two and two together. During the board meeting, they realized they were making big mistakes that needed to be corrected immediately. In this meeting, they had already defined actions to reevaluate the Rule of Three and realign their incoherent marketing, HR, and operations strategies.

Oscar: I knew you had potential and would do a good job. Now I'm not the only one. We also have the support of the other boards to continue our work. Congratulations!

Me: Thank you. I don't know what to say. I didn't think I was doing anything important—it hasn't brought any innovation yet.

Oscar: Remember that to innovate is to generate more value with the available resources. You've identified points of improvement that will bring huge savings.

I was thrilled that I had contributed positively to the company's results. Even without providing a solution to the problems, just identifying them was seen as a significant contribution. I discovered that many problems aren't so difficult to solve if they're diagnosed accurately and at the right time. The problem is when they go unnoticed or are simply ill-defined, leading to the development of misguided solutions and the need to redo work.

Oscar told me that my department transfer had been formalized and that I would move to the position of innovation analyst, almost doubling my salary. Obviously, I didn't complain, but I confess that I was so motivated that I would have continued doing my job even if the salary had decreased.

Oscar: Actually, I think you deserve to earn more than that, considering the savings your work will bring... However, HR salary policies are pretty restrictive.

Me: Yes. The bank is full of rules. I know. But I'm happy with the new position and salary. It's more than I expected.

Oscar: Modesty!

He smiled and gave me a high-five. I felt it was a thank you for bringing home a win for his department—a victory he needed.

I showed him a summary of the behaviors for the different mindsets I had mapped out so far.

Output-Driven	Outcome-Driven
Rigid I resist change and avoid new ideas.	**Adaptable** I always challenge the status quo.
Obedient I follow explicit instructions without question.	**Creative** I figure out how to achieve the best result.
Individualistic I ignore other points of view.	**Collaborative** I take responsibility for collaboration and shared understanding.

Oscar: I like how you synthesized all these behaviors into a table by presenting them as opposites. It makes the differences very clear.

Me: I know it's not binary, like 0 and 1. I mean, I'm sure there's a whole scale of behavior levels between one extreme and the other, but this structure helps us understand the behaviors we want to replicate to foster an innovative corporate culture.

Oscar: It seems that you're already assuming outcome-driven behavior. How can we get the rest of the company to do the same? Do you think we could clone you?

I remembered my mindset conversation with Barbara, the senior business analyst, when she said, "What we think and feel shapes our actions."

> Me: This table shows a good map of behaviors, but our mindset is still incomplete. To change behaviors, we first need to change the invisible part of the mindset: thoughts and feelings. Can I investigate a little more?

> Oscar: Sure. You've already earned a place of trust, and I look forward to seeing what else you come up with.

From the interviews I had already conducted, I had some clues about how people thought and felt in the company. However, I wanted to validate my hypotheses and conclude my diagnosis before proposing a solution for transforming the entire company's corporate culture. Until then, I had no idea where to start.

Chapter 17: Test Score

I returned to the Call Center to face a ghost from the past: Mr. Andrade. His behavior was very output-driven, and I wanted to understand his thoughts and why he acted the way he did. I sent an email, and he accepted the first appointment I suggested.

When I entered the department, I saw several colleagues and passed by Rodrigo's desk.

Rodrigo: Well, look who's here! To what do we owe the honor?

Me: Just dropping by to say hi. I have an appointment with Mr. Andrade in a minute. How are you?

Rodrigo: I'm great. I've just started an evening course in Asian cooking, and I love it. You have to see the new recipes I've learned.

Me: Um... I'd love to. Let's have dinner at the weekend. Can I bring a friend?

Rodrigo: Friend?!

His eyes widened with surprise.

Rodrigo: Of course you can! It will be a pleasure. Looks like you're finally living life, huh?

Me: I am.

I smiled proudly and thought about the transformation of my life since leaving the Call Center. I looked around and didn't feel any nostalgia for my past existence in that place. Taking a deeper look at my transformation, I realized that it wasn't the department or the job itself that was the reason for my unhappiness while working there. I was responsible for making my life miserable because of how I behaved. I didn't just change departments. I changed myself.

Rodrigo: What are you going to talk about with "Swamp Thing"?

We had been in the habit of referring to Mr. Andrade with less-than-affectionate nicknames. Badmouthing the boss and work seemed to be standard behavior in our corporate culture. Everyone did it, and we learned by imitation. I confess it's pretty liberating to find fault with the boss and blame him for work hassles. By blaming our problems on the hierarchical structure at work, we can absolve ourselves of any responsibility.

Me: I'm going to try to understand how he thinks.

Rodrigo: He thinks?

That was our admiration for the boss—trashing him behind his back but being polite and submissive to his face. Now I would talk to him from a different viewpoint; I was no longer his employee but a colleague from another department.

I walked into his office, and he made a point of getting up to greet me.

> Mr. Andrade: The prodigal son returns! You abandoned us, and I heard about it from your new director's secretary. Couldn't you have told me yourself?

> Me: I'm sorry about that. It was all so fast and unexpected that I didn't even have time to come and talk to you.

> Mr. Andrade: Well, there's no need for formalities. Please, call me Bob.

I didn't expect him to be so approachable. None of the Call Center employees called Mr. Andrade by his first name, let alone a nickname. They always treated him with formality and reverence. What had changed?

> Mr. Andrade: I understand you're in another area now and looking for other kinds of results. I'm glad you were able to find a good opportunity here at the company. Grab it tooth and nail and stay focused. That's how I moved up the career ladder. I don't think working as a call center agent was really your thing.

> Me: I don't think my contribution to the performance indicators was the best in the team.

> Mr. Andrade: Don't be so modest. It was undisputedly the worst.

He burst out laughing, and I didn't know whether I was meant to feel proud or ashamed. I'd never much cared for Call Center performance indicators. They diverted us from outcomes and committed us solely to outputs. Horrendous! It made my stomach churn just thinking about the practice of dropping calls to reduce the Average Handle Time. I didn't understand how anyone could be complicit in this practice or, even worse, encourage it, as Mr. Andrade did. His mindset was undoubtedly very different from mine.

> Mr. Andrade: Anyway, in the department you're in now, the indicators will be different, and you'll be able to perform better. The important thing is that you make sure you're aligned with your department's goals and perform them to the best of your ability.

> Me: Is that how you became a call center manager?

> Mr. Andrade: You can bet it is. I started out as an agent like you, but I soon understood the impact that performance indicators could have on my career. I was always the agent who got the best indicators, which got me promoted to manager. In this position, I implemented policies and procedures that improved the indicators of the entire department, and today, we're a reference in quality. I know my employees see me as a slave driver, but I need to be demanding to maintain the standard of quality that we have achieved. I think you can understand that.

I was surprised to find that I did understand. Although I disagreed with his rationale, I must admit that Mr.

Andrade had successfully delivered what was expected of his department, or at least as far as his contract described it. Local goal-setting works as a contract between the company and the department manager. The output-driven manager delivers his goals and doesn't even look at the overall results. Concern for the bigger picture isn't part of their responsibilities.

At heart, Mr. Andrade wasn't a bad person or someone who wasn't committed to the company. He was a professional who was highly dedicated to his department's success. His grumpy, disagreeable manner and the seemingly irrational policies that led to customer dissatisfaction were nothing more than strategies he had created to meet the terms of his contract. If measured by these indicators alone, we could say that his strategies worked.

I wondered how many managers I would find with the same profile. Dozens, hundreds, thousands. I tried to put myself in his place and realized I had often behaved that way, thinking only of local indicators and ignoring the bigger picture. As a student, I spent many nights before an exam memorizing formulas and concepts to use the next day, only to forget them immediately afterward. Nor can I deny that I copied my neighbors' responses quite a few times. My commitment was not to learning but to grading.

I thanked Mr. Andrade for the conversation and left, understanding a little better how he thought and why he behaved the way he did.

Now I needed to find a different pattern of behavior and

another way of thinking to compare it to. I remembered someone who didn't simply comply with their area's service level agreements, and I surprised myself when I asked for his help.

Remember Oswald in Legal? I went to talk to him again. Something told me he didn't have a "follow the herd" mindset. He wouldn't have helped me help Oscar if he wasn't outcome-driven. Maybe he could help me better understand how the people at the bank thought and what needed to change.

I didn't just show up this time but scheduled a formal interview. I arrived with a box of chocolates.

> Oswald: Uh-oh. Come to grease my palm again, have you?

He laughed and opened the box right away so we could share the chocolates while talking.

> Oswald: Thank you for the sweetener. I've heard you're working in the Innovation Department and doing very well there. Congratulations!

The news was spreading. I hadn't spoken to Oswald again and I didn't expect him to remember me as anything other than some crazy guy from the Call Center who had bothered him one day. The fact that he knew something about what I was doing made me think that I must be making some impact on the organization. I felt a mixture of pride, vanity, and the weight of responsibility. Knowing that they were following my movements gave me butterflies in my stomach.

Me: Thank you! I've been talking to many people and trying to understand the corporate culture here at the bank.

Oswald: What have you discovered?

Me: In a nutshell, people are only committed to what they have to deliver and don't care about the impact of their work on the overall result.

Oswald: Bingo! You said it all! You have accurately summed up the people who work in our company and practically all the employees of every company in the world.

He put a whole chocolate into his mouth and opened another one.

Oswald: The world would be much better if people would look beyond the end of their noses.

Me: But not everyone acts like that. You, for example.

Oswald: Gracious me, I appreciate the vote of confidence! In truth, I'm just a stubborn old man who won't give up his beliefs.

Me: And what are those beliefs?

Oswald: Well, despite appearances, I was once a strapping youth with a full head of hair, and when I was young, I studied a lot of Eastern philosophies such as Taoism, Hinduism, Pantheism, and Buddhism. I never became a devout religious type, mind you, but I always sought a more holistic vision to understand the world.

In other words, I recognize the interdependence of all beings and the phenomena that surround us, and I believe that human decisions should take into account the well-being of all forms of life.

The contrast between Oswald's and Mr. Andrade's ways of thinking highlighted the difference in their mindsets, which I noted as follows:

Output-Driven Mindset

- **Limited:** I worry about my own success.

Outcome-Driven Mindset

- **Holistic:** I understand value for everyone.

Chapter 18: The Flow of Purple Folders

I asked Oswald if he knew of examples that exemplified the limited thinking of the output-driven mindset and why we need to change it.

> Oswald: I'll give you a hint: Follow the flow of the purple folders!

I felt like Dorothy in *The Wizard of Oz*.

> Me: Follow the purple folders?

> Oswald: Yes. Go to Accounting and ask for the flow of the purple folders. It's something so ingrained in how the bank works that no one questions it. Then tell me what you find out, just between you and me.

While investigating this kind of "anonymous complaint," I met Adelaide, the accounting manager responsible for a team of analysts involved in the mysterious flow of purple folders.

> Adelaide: I'm happy to help the Innovation Department.

We're very innovative here and always seek excellence in our work.

Adelaide was a woman in her mid-thirties. She was very well groomed in a rather austere manner, with not a hair out of place. She wore glasses and had the habit of blinking rapidly before speaking. She seemed extremely committed to her work and proud of her results.

Adelaide: We haven't had a single delay in delivering the purple folders for years. Even though the volume of data has tripled, we've been able to adapt the team and our internal processes to comply with our service level agreement.

Me: What an excellent performance! I'm sorry if the question I'm going to ask is too basic, but I'm still getting familiar with this process, and I think you might be able to help me. What is a purple folder?

Adelaide: Oh, you don't know! The purple folder is a report that describes and analyzes all payments made by the bank the previous day. Any payment, whether it's an employee's salary, purchase of office supplies, plane tickets, property rental, property security service, job posting in classifieds... everything the bank paid for is described and compiled in the purple folder for that day.

Me: All the payments from all the departments?

Adelaide: Everything! Be it a department, branch, or service station. If the bank paid that day, it's in the purple folder.

The volume of information seemed like something that should be in a digital information system. I asked her if it was a real folder, a physical document with numbers printed on it, and she confirmed that it was. The documentation compiled information from one system and several expense control systems in different areas. The accounting team validated each piece of information, checked invoices and receipts, and checked the statement of accounts before gathering all the information in the purple folder of the day.

Me: Can I see a purple folder?

Adelaide: Sure. I'll grab the one we're preparing today for you to look at. It's still incomplete, but you'll have an idea.

I confess that I was surprised when Adelaide came back with a black cardboard folder in her hand. She passed it to me and I saw a sticker on the cover with the title *Purple Folder* and the previous day's date.

Me: How ignorant of me! I thought purple was the color of the folder, not an acronym. What does it stand for? Payment Update Report for Processing...? What do the L and the E stand for?

Adelaide: They don't mean anything. You were right. Purple was just the color of the folder. It's supposed to be called the Daily Report of Payments Made, but many years ago, when they started producing this report, they used to forward it to the finance department in a purple folder. So, everyone started calling it the purple folder, and the name stuck. No one uses any other term to refer to this report.

Me: But the folder isn't purple.

Adelaide: For a long time, it was, but it was getting harder to find purple folders. For a few years, the bank even signed a contract with a supplier that guaranteed the delivery of purple folders and produced them exclusively for our use. This exclusivity was expensive, and the cost of each purple folder was much higher than that of other folders you can easily find in a stationery store. The switch to black folders with a label was an innovation we implemented, which brought significant savings.

Strange how things evolve and how some "innovations" look more like Dr. Frankenstein's monster. I opened the folder and saw that it contained reports extracted from an accounting system laser-printed on glossy magazine paper.

Adelaide: We had to invest in a more modern printer to print at the quality standard that the analysts in the Finance Department demand. As the volume of pages has been increasing, this printer needs a high productivity index. Now, we have a top-of-the-line printer.

Me: Do you generate this report every day based on the previous day's payments?

Adelaide: Yes. Often, the areas are slow to make information available, and we need to work a few extra hours to deliver on time, but we never let it go to the next day.

I was impressed by the standard of excellence with which Adelaide and her team worked to deliver the black folders labeled purple. But I remembered Oswald's advice to go with the "flow," so I decided to ask what happens to the purple folders when they're ready.

Adelaide: The purple folders are forwarded to Finance.

I discovered that the folders were placed in a mail pouch in the Accounting Department's exit bin at the end of the day for delivery to the Finance Department, which would use the information.

A specific and highly efficient department manages the transit of pouches in the bank. It's like an internal post office with postmen who pass through all the exit bins daily, collecting envelopes, boxes, and letters and taking them to their destination, which are entry bins in other locations. Early every morning, one of these professionals transported the purple folder from the Accounting Department to the Finance Department.

I was surprised to realize that, in the entrance bin of the Finance Department, the purple folder delivered that day was not alone but stacked on top of three other purple folders delivered over the previous days. I talked to a financial analyst to understand this next stage of the flow.

Me: How important are purple folders?

Financial Analyst: They contain information essential for the cash flow control we do here in Finance.

Me: Do you do this daily? I noticed that three folders are stacked in the input bin.

Financial Analyst: Well noted. The purple folders are processed weekly. We accumulate the folders for the week and send everything to be scanned on Friday.

Me: To be scanned?

Financial Analyst: Yes. An outsourced company scans the reports from the purple folders and translates the images into high-quality data. In the past, we tried to do this in-house, but the quality was very poor and generated a lot of rework. Today, with better print resolution and the work of this specialized company, we hardly ever have problems.

If you didn't doze off in the last few paragraphs and managed to go with the flow of the purple folders with me, you must be as shocked as I was. Let me recap: Accounting paid overtime to transform digital data into an analog document every day, which would pile up until the end of the week before it was scanned and converted back into digital form, including possible errors. And someone boasted that this process reduced rework.

My head almost exploded when I learned this. It's fair enough that implementing change takes energy and people tend to resist change to save energy, but what I was seeing was a motherlode of wasted energy. People had even made changes in search of optimization but with a view too restricted to their department or function. It was apparent that no one had looked at the flow from beginning to end.

This whole process could be made simpler and faster merely by interconnecting the Accounting and Finance systems.

Maybe my vision was still limited. Maybe the purple folders were used for something else after the scan, which would at least justify their printing. I asked about their destination.

Me: What happens after the purple folders are scanned?

Financial Analyst: I don't know. I'll give you the details of the company that does the scanning, and you can ask them.

I continued my journey on the trail of the purple folders, a tad apprehensive about what I might find. I discovered that after the folders were scanned, the outsourced company reviewed the scanned data again, which often required manual adjustments. The folders were then stored for a month in the company's local deposit in case they needed to review data questioned by the financial analysts.

On a monthly basis, the folders were moved from the company's deposit to the records storage facility controlled by the Inventory Department, where the physical files were kept. I even visited this stock and found hundreds of bookshelves with thousands of purple (and black) folders perfectly cataloged and organized sequentially in chronological sections. I talked with the archivist about them.

Me: How long should these folders be stored before they can be disposed of?

Archivist: Indefinitely. Like many other documents here, this is an expanding archive. We're already renting a new building to extend the records storage facility because this one's reaching total capacity.

Me: Hmmm. One last question. How often does someone come here to look at one of these purple folders?

Archivist: Since I've been working here, never.

Me: How long have you been working here?

Archivist: Thirteen years.

And that is the final step in the purple folder flow. I felt like Dorothy when she finally reached the end of the yellow brick road and met the so-called Wizard of Oz. Far from Adelaide's pride in her prompt and "excellent," as she put it, delivery, the flow of purple folders led to a similarly unworthy ending. They weren't just a monumental waste of resources. They were totally unnecessary.

This led me to uncover two additional differences between the two mindsets, which I wrote down:

Output-Driven Mindset

- **Compliant:** I am responsible for doing things right.

Outcome-Driven Mindset

- **Effective:** I am responsible for making sure the right things get done.

I realized that many people were doing the wrong thing right. It wasn't out of ill intent or lack of commitment. It was because they started from a mistaken belief. If they had a more holistic view, considering the whole instead of just their area or function, they would realize that there are other, more effective ways to achieve the expected outputs.

I felt a sting of sadness at the thought of writing this in a report and exposing such a painfully embarrassing situation. It would surely demand changes to a complex structure. Changes in indicators, policies, processes, systems, and leadership would be necessary to optimize the flow of purple folders and Call Center service.

I remembered that everyone was watching me, and I confess that I felt a little intimidated by all this complexity. Would it be better to sweep everything under the carpet and leave things as they were?

After lunch, I would tell Oswald what I had discovered and ask for his opinion. But before that, I had a meeting with someone special.

Chapter 19: Dona Rosa's Charm

At lunchtime, I went to the post office near work to meet Julia. We had arranged to pick up her magic kit from China and have a snack.

> Julia: Thanks for coming with me. I don't want to cause any trouble.

> Me: It's no trouble at all. I work right next door. It'll be a pleasure to stand in line with you.

Whenever I met Julia, it was like... you know that feeling when you move into an environment and everything suddenly gets better? Like on a blazing hot summer day, when you step into a cool, air-conditioned room. Or, after hours on a cramped, sweaty bus, when you suddenly disembark on a breathtaking beachfront? Or if you were almost drowning, desperate to breathe, and suddenly reached the sweet air at the surface? That's how I felt when I saw her. The colors and soundtrack of my story shifted. Today, she looked beautiful wearing the same white buttoned shirt and gray skirt she wore to work at school. She was stunning in any outfit. Unfortunately, we were both on our lunch break and didn't have much time.

I only came out of my enchantment when I looked at the post office door and noticed that the old lady with the toy guitar wasn't there. I had never seen her again since giving her the money from Dona Rosa's charm. An otherworldly feeling sent a shiver down my spine. I decided to tell the story to Julia while we were waiting in line, and she wanted to know more about the so-called charm.

Julia: What kind of money was it? Did you say it was a kind of charm?

Me: Yes. I had already forgotten about it when I found it folded deep inside, behind my ID card. It had been hidden in my wallet for several years. It was one of Dona Rosa's charms.

Julia: Who's Dona Rosa?

Me: The mother of a neighbor who lived near my parents. Every January 6th, his family celebrated Three Kings Day in honor of the Three Wise Men, who, according to the Bible, brought gifts to the baby Jesus. One year, I was invited. After dinner, we said some prayers, and Dona Rosa gave us each three mustard seeds. She made us take a bill of money from our wallets. We had to fold the bill with those little seeds inside, put it back in our wallets, and leave it there for at least a year without touching it. After that time, we couldn't spend that money—we had to give it to someone who needed it. Those were the instructions of the charm. A year passed—two, three, five, I don't know how many—and I forgot about the money. Then I found it again one day and gave it to the old lady who used to sing at the post office door.

Julia: And what was the purpose of this charm?

Me: I don't remember exactly. I think it was to help you make money or be successful, something like that.

Julia: Well, then, it worked. Didn't you tell me you got a raise and you're doing well at work?

Me: Yes, that's true. I thought about that, too. But all this change wasn't the result of magic or a charm. It was the result of a change in my behavior. And I changed my behavior deliberately, based on my logical thoughts and feelings.

Julia: I don't see why one thing can't be linked to another. Maybe everything's connected. The charm might need a change of attitude to come true, or it might have influenced your subsequent attitudes.

Me: It sounds complicated.

Julia: And for the person who receives the money, what's the expected outcome of the charm?

Me: I have no idea, and it gives me the heebie-jeebies. I don't know what happened to the old lady. Do you think I did her any harm?

Julia: Have you asked Dona Rosa if the charm affects

the person who receives the money?

Me: Dona Rosa died shortly after that Three Kings Day, and the neighbor moved away. I'm scared to look into it. These supernatural things give me the creeps.

Julia: I think they're fascinating. I love the story! We should look for the old lady and find out what happened to her. Did she realize that the money had some little seeds inside? I wonder what impact it's had on her life. Let's investigate!

This girl was a find. Talk about courage! There was I, quaking in my boots just thinking about Dona Rosa's charm, and next to me, Julia, cool as a cucumber, was all set for a ghost hunt. The situation resembled the Chinese-made magic kit we were about to pick up. We know that, behind the magic, there's a cheap and usually simple trick. There's no magic—it's all illusion. But when the kids see the trick, they're all astonished. The story of Dona Rosa's charm was like another magic show—Julia was willing to enjoy every moment innocently without prejudging.

Finally, we got to the front of the line and picked up the package, which we didn't even have time to open. We had to grab a hot dog from a cart in the square to get back in time.

Me: That hot dog doesn't count. I still owe you a proper meal.

Julia: No way! It's great. You don't owe me anything.

She wasn't getting it. The indebtedness was just an excuse to be able to meet her again. If I could, I would meet with her every day. I loved her company and wanted much more. She might shy away from me if she found out about my feelings and didn't feel the same. I decided to risk an invitation to another outing. To avoid the connotation of a romantic encounter that might spook her, I put it casually.

> Me: I have a friend who's taking an Asian cooking course and needs guinea pigs to test his recipes on. I'm going to his house for dinner this Saturday, and he's asked me to bring someone to get a second opinion. Would you like to go with me?

> Julia: Ooh, I love Asian food. Count me in!

Phew! It worked. I would have another opportunity to meet her, deepen our friendship, and, who knows, nurture something more romantic. Talk about swimming in insecurity!

Chapter 20: Ego

In the afternoon, I went back to tell Oswald everything I had discovered by following the flow of the purple folders.

Oswald: My God! I knew purple folders hadn't made sense since they computerized the Finance system, but I never imagined they were that wasteful.

Me: How did you know?

Oswald: Many years ago, I was asked to support the Finance Department in a project to review budget forecasting policies. At the time, they were creating a system that would automate a set of rules using information from these purple folders. I found it odd that they used paper information and suggested that they integrate the financial and accounting systems. It seemed an obvious step.

Me: But they didn't listen to you.

Oswald: Worse than that. They gave me an earful and

told me to stick to my job of reviewing the policies. The finance manager at the time didn't even want to hear about integration with Accounting.

Me: Why?

Oswald: Apparently, the accounting and finance managers didn't get along very well. Each had a different view of how things should be done, and they thought it best to keep their noses out of each other's business. It's like two aggressive dogs whose bowls are side by side. If both eat from their own bowls and keep to themselves, everything's fine. But if one of them looks to the side, all hell breaks loose!

That's how the flow of the purple folders came to be. The managers created restrictions for the flow of information, and each wanted to ensure dominance in their own territory, regardless of what happened on the other side of the fence.

I tried talking to the managers involved about the problems I had identified, but the responses were distinctly antagonistic.

Problem? We don't have a problem here. We're a benchmark for quality in our work.

We've always done it this way.

We're doing exactly what has been asked of us. If they don't know how to use what we deliver, that's not my problem.

If the other area has a problem, let them solve it. I don't get paid to solve other people's problems.

We know what we need to do and always deliver in the best

possible way. If we have to keep having alignment meetings with other departments, we'll spend the day discussing the number of sprinkles on a doughnut and won't get our jobs done.

Are you trying to tell me how I should do my job? I'm an expert on this and you're just a kid who doesn't know how things work around here. You'd better mind your own business!

Interestingly, the managers' attitudes were now very different. Initially, when I was asking them what they did and how they worked, they were all proud and smiling, showing off their medals and victories. "We're innovators," they said. Now that I came to present an outside view and point out the problems and the need to implement changes, the atmosphere had soured, and no one seemed interested in listening to me.

I knew that people like to be heard but don't have much patience for listening. People are self-centered, but I noticed that this individualism was even more pronounced in the case of managers. They had an aversion to opinions differing from their own. When a problem was pointed out, they felt offended and tried to pass the blame on to others. They didn't want outside interference and despised ideas that they themselves hadn't thought of.

In my opinion, these weren't people who lacked commitment. It wasn't that. Each manager defends their area with all their might, but who stands up for the company?

I noticed a huge difference between how directors and managers deal with the problems I identified. When I talked to the marketing, operations, and HR directors, they soon realized they needed to change and redirect their actions. At least that's what Oscar told me had happened at the board meeting. The managers, on the other hand, closed the doors of their castles and placed their archers on top of the ramparts, their arrows pointing at me.

Directors have a strategic vision (as expected) and meet periodically to discuss the organization's strategy. Managers from different areas do not have such meetings. Each one is guided by their director and meets with their team of subordinates to fulfill tasks. They operate with a strictly local vision and have a service provider culture that "never says no."

Is decreasing Handling Time in the Call Center the goal? Consider it diminished.

Do you need better print quality? Of course, we'll arrange it.

More space to store documents? We're already renting some.

A given task is a completed task. We're super committed.

However, the commitment is to the task's output, not the outcome. Committing to the outcome would require questioning what was asked of them, understanding the reasons, validating that the deliverables are the most appropriate for that situation, and taking responsibility for results that go beyond their area of expertise.

How will this goal impact our customer satisfaction?

Why do they need better print quality?

What's the use of these documents you want to store?

Is this task the most appropriate to achieve the expected outcomes?

It's much more comfortable for a manager and their team to follow orders without question and hold others accountable for the organization's poor results. The responsibility of looking at the strategy remains exclusive to the directors. But directors take a long time to learn what's happening and respond, and they generally don't have all the operational information. What's more, the way directors convey strategy to their managers is limited to the impact of their department. As a result, the vision of the whole is not shared from the top down or from the bottom up.

I added another mindset component to my notebook, but this time, it wasn't related to how people act or think but to what they feel.

Output-Driven Mindset

- **Averse to debate:** I have no patience for differing opinions.

Outcome-Driven Mindset

- **Open to listening:** I am sensitive to different personalities and their unique needs.

I'll admit that I wasn't expecting this response from the managers, and I was unsettled by their reaction when I tried to convince them that changes would be needed in their areas.

Although I didn't yet have much experience in the role I was taking on, I very much wanted to succeed in my mission to change the corporate culture. Until then, I hadn't realized I might suffer reprisals from those who wanted to maintain the status quo. I was afraid. Should I keep going?

Chapter 21: To the Rhythm of Complexity

At night, lying in bed, I kept thinking about these fears. Fear of the supernatural, fear of declaring myself and losing Julia's friendship, fear of saying that Call Center performance indicators generate customer dissatisfaction and being accused of being a traitor, fear of exposing the wasteful flow of purple folders and provoking an organizational revolution that would impact many people's work. It was fear of complexity and change.

Many people live in fear. It's natural for them to be cautious before committing to a change. Change brings uncertainty, and uncertainty is a risk. In general, people prefer stability and predictability. But when fear is paralyzing, people can become trapped in unhealthy situations.

Suddenly, I felt a nudge on my shoulder. I looked to the side, and it was Adelaide, holding a red folder with a label that read *Green Folder.*

Adelaide: We've decided to change everything around

here. Our commitment to excellence never stops, and now, instead of purple folders, we'll deliver green folders.

Me: But why will the documents continue to be printed? Data exchange between systems would be much simpler and avoid so much waste. Changing to stay the same way doesn't help.

Adelaide: Do you have any idea how much this printer cost? How will we justify its purchase if we stop printing these reports? What about the contract of the outsourced company that scans the documents? We've already signed a contract for one year of services. What am I going to say to them?

Me: But I thought...

Adelaide: Your problem is that you think too much. You can't think of everything. Take this folder straight to the marketing director, who is urgently waiting for the report.

Holding the briefcase, I entered an elevator and exited directly into Mello's room.

Me: I think this is for you.

Mello: Great! That was just the report I needed to justify our new marketing investment.

Me: The payroll report?

Mello: No! The Call Center's indicators.

Mello opened the red folder titled green and showed indicators that the bank's Call Center service is the best not only among companies in the financial sector but also worldwide.

Mello: Our Call Center provides excellent service and is among the best in the world. We'll eliminate all other service channels and keep only the Call Center. We'll be an international benchmark for quality.

He couldn't be talking about the same call center where I had worked. I knew those indicators and that the numbers hid dropped calls and unhappy customers. The Call Center didn't have the built-in systems needed to serve customers; mostly, it referred them to resolve their issues at the branch. That wouldn't be an innovation but a step backward. I needed someone to help me get Mello to give up on this idea.

Rodrigo was making a mushroom omelet in the coffee corner, and I ran over to ask him for help.

Me: Rodrigo, we need to solve this problem.

Rodrigo: Who, me?! Get lost! We don't get paid to solve problems. We get paid to follow the script.

The omelet smelled good, and a line began to form, with people holding plates and waiting for a piece. I saw Oswald from the Legal Department in the middle of the line and went to talk to him.

Oswald: Is this the chocolate line?

Me: I don't know. I think it's for an omelet or coffee. I'm not sure.

Oswald: I've heard you're good at repairing coffee machines. Congratulations! The Legal Department's coffee machine is broken. Stop by to fix it for us.

Rodrigo tapped me on the shoulder and pulled me aside.

Rodrigo: I told you! "Every initiative will be severely punished!" Now you'll have to repair the coffee machines for all the departments.

Was that my fate? My fear was rising. Things were too complicated, and I felt utterly unprepared to handle it all. I didn't have the proper training or experience for this role. I was just some guy Oscar had taken a crazy risk on. As I remembered Oscar, I noticed him by my side. We were standing in front of an orchestra of musicians, instruments at the ready and waiting for a cue. They included a pianist, violinists, cellists, percussionists, trumpeters, and a whole bunch of others whose instruments I don't even know the name of. There was quite a crowd! Behind the orchestra was a huge sign with the symphony title in capital letters: *COMPLEXITY.*

Oscar: Here's the baton. Now you must conduct the orchestra.

Me: Are you crazy?! I have no idea how to do that.

Behind me, all the bank employees were seated in an auditorium waiting for the show. I started sweating. My legs trembled, and I barely had the strength to lift my arms. I saw that the musicians had the score before them, and I hoped they knew what to do. I motioned to start, and they began to play an atrocious attempt at the "Funeral March." People snickered and whispered in the audience about my failure. It was mortifying!

Mercifully, the orchestra ground to a halt. I was considering faking a faint to escape my predicament when Oscar brought someone to help me. It was Barbara, the senior business analyst.

> Barbara: A band can only work if everyone plays the same song. You're not playing the right music.

> Me: This "Complexity" stuff is scary. I don't know how to lead people like you do. I don't have your experience.

> Barbara: You will learn, and experience will come with time, but right now, you have to deal with this. You need to learn how to conduct "Complexity."

> Me: But I don't know what comes next. I'm scared.

> Barbara: Don't think of it that way. Think about all the things you're learning and how much more you're going to learn.

> Me: I like learning.

> Barbara: I know. Run with that! Feel motivated by challenges. They're like a game where you beat the levels and move forward. Think of them positively. Complexity is live music—stimulating and seductive.

I looked at the orchestra with fresh eyes. The title *COMPLEXITY* behind the musicians didn't scare me anymore. I felt tremendously curious to discover how the song would play out. I raised my arms, now confident and ready to conduct the orchestra. The musicians waited for my signal. I remembered the school band's *tum-tum* and thought, "My role is to provide the musical pulse and let the musicians shine with their instruments."

I set the tempo, and the orchestra started again, but this time, the tune was different—a tango by Astor Piazzolla. They played divinely, and I felt inspired by the music. It wasn't a simple melody. It was complex, full of nuances, with highs and lows, and very sensual. The audience was silent at the beginning but applauded when a couple entered the stage, dancing the tango behind me.

I couldn't see the dancers properly because I was watching the musicians in the orchestra, attentive to my conducting role, which, miraculously, I seemed able to do. Even so, I could see that it was a rather peculiar couple. The man was big and heavy, and the woman was tiny. This enabled him to execute acrobatic moves with relative ease, propelling her from side to side as she performed the steps with lightness and precision.

I couldn't resist, so I turned my eyes to get a better look at the dancers and realized they were two people I knew. The man was Mr. Andrade, and the woman was the old homeless lady who now had her guitar in her hand and began to sing:

> *Let life take me, life takes me...*
> *I am happy and grateful for all that God gave me.*

That was too much. I woke up. The sight of those two dancing was wackier than any dream I'd ever had. My imagination had truly outdone itself!

I spent a few seconds trying to remember the dream and how my mind was trying to organize the experiences I'd been living, to connect them so I could understand not only the thoughts but also the feelings involved. I grabbed my notebook and wrote down the differences I noticed in the default feelings of each mindset when faced with the complexity of life.

Output-Driven Mindset

- **Fearful:** I feel uncomfortable when there is ambiguity or uncertainty.

Outcome-Driven Mindset

- **Bold:** I love learning new things. Challenges motivate me.

I looked at the clock. It was late, but not too late. I called Julia and was lucky to catch her still awake.

Me: I have something important to tell you. Can I go down to your place?

Julia: Sure.

I went downstairs to her apartment and told her how I felt. I told her that I loved her friendship and that, if I could, I would spend much more time with her. I told her how fascinated I was by her beauty, kindness, and attitude toward life and how she inspired me to be a better person. Finally, I said I would like to be more than her friend. She said nothing but gazed into my eyes for a few seconds, before responding with our first kiss.

Chapter 22: Transcendental Sushi

We arrived at Rodrigo's house early Saturday evening. When he opened the door, he noticed that Julia and I were holding hands and shot me a knowing look and a mischievous smile.

Me: Hey Rodrigo. This is my girlfriend, Julia.

Rodrigo: Nice to meet you.

Julia: Likewise.

The mischievous smile became an expression of respect. It was the first time I had publicly introduced Julia as my girlfriend. I felt that the word "girlfriend" had a certain weight of commitment, and I enjoyed introducing her like that. I was proud and full of admiration for the beautiful girl who smiled and chatted freely. Being Julia's boyfriend was certainly the biggest of my successes until then.

Julia: I hear you're taking an Asian cooking course and need some guinea pigs.

Rodrigo: Yep. I made a few dishes today and added a personal touch to the recipes I learned in the course. I hope you like them.

Me: I'm sure we will. Rodrigo's an excellent cook, and he's very creative.

We sat down at the table, and Rodrigo went off to get something. I offered to help, and, in the kitchen, he nudged me on the arm, speaking softly so Julia wouldn't hear.

Rodrigo: You didn't tell me you were dating!

Me: Last time I saw you, I wasn't.

Rodrigo: She's cute! Don't let her get away.

Me: I'll do my best.

We went back to the living room. I was carrying some cocktails based on sake and berries that Rodrigo had made earlier, and he bore a little tray with three pots of red fish mixed with onions, pepper chips, and many other things I couldn't identify. He announced the dish as if announcing a star's entrance to the stage.

Rodrigo: To begin, we have an amuse-bouche: an appetizer with fresh tuna tartar, *massago*, and the citrus touch of *yuzu*.

I think the *massago* was the little balls on top of the fish. I have no idea what *yuzu* is, but the taste was phenomenal.

Julia: Wow! This is divine!

Me: Get ready. If I know our chef, he's just getting started.

Rodrigo returned from the kitchen with a beautiful tray of patterned porcelain holding something in thin slices covered with sauce.

> Rodrigo: Carpaccio of finely sliced scallops, drizzled with homemade ponzu sauce and finished with fleur de sel.

Another explosion of flavors. I don't think I've ever eaten anything so delicious. Julia closed her eyes as she put each slice in her mouth to savor that experience and let out small sighs of bliss.

> Me: Rodrigo, my friend, you're wasting your time at the Call Center. You should work in gastronomy. This is your true talent!

> Rodrigo: I've already told you. Gastronomy is not my job. It's recreation, and I don't want to spoil it. Leave things as they are!

> Julia: It's so good! This food is absolutely delicious.

> Rodrigo: I haven't brought out my boldest bet of the night yet. I want to give you a transcendental experience.

He went to the kitchen and lingered a little longer this time, finishing the dish with some element that had to be prepared at the last minute.

> Rodrigo: The next dish should be savored carefully. I call it the "Ephemeral Zen Garden." It consists of white fish sashimi with Sakura flower jelly and a flavor-changing sauce.

He served a bed of delicately sliced white fish sashimi on a dark tray. On the sashimi, a clear gelatin infused with Sakura flower was slowly melting at room temperature.

Me: What's that sauce on top? It looks different!

Rodrigo: This is my magic sauce, a special sauce that changes flavor when interacting with Sakura gelatin. The sauce starts with a mild citrus flavor, and as the gelatin melts, it transforms, taking on sweeter, more floral notes.

The dish was arranged to resemble a Zen Garden, with elements such as stones, sand, and vegetation represented by ingredients such as fine herbs, pink peppercorns, and small edible flowers.

Julia: It really is transcendental! As the sauce mixes with the gelatin, the flavor changes. It's like several dishes in one.

Rodrigo: I'm glad you noticed that.

As the dish transformed, we observed the visual changes and tasted the variations in flavor and texture. The dish not only offered us a unique dining experience but invited us on a journey of transformation, reflecting the fleeting beauty and constant change of nature.

Me: If the dish you made can be transformed, why can't you, Rodrigo? You should at least try a culinary profession. It is, after all, your true calling.

Rodrigo: It's too risky! I have a stable job at the bank.

Julia: I've decided that I'm going to change. It's inspiring to see that you've taken a course and that you're developing your talents this way. I've had my eye on a course for a therapeutic companion and wasn't sure if I should invest time and money in it, but after tasting your food, I've decided. I want to transcend as well.

I didn't expect this one! I knew that Rodrigo didn't like working in the bank's Call Center and that a change could be positive in his life, but I had the impression that Julia felt fulfilled at her job and wasn't looking for a change of direction.

Me: I thought you were happy as a teaching assistant.

Julia: I am, but things can always be better. One of the children in the morning class is autistic. He's a lovely, sweet boy but very hard to deal with. He lives in his own world and needs attention almost all the time. I'm doing my best, but I feel unprepared to deal with him. I saw the course a few weeks ago and was interested.

Rodrigo: Do you think it's worth investing in?

Julia: Absolutely. It offers a certificate that qualifies me to work as a therapeutic companion. I'd love to do it and could earn a lot more than I do as just a teacher.

I remembered a phrase I had heard from the operations manager: "If it ain't broke, don't fix it." Julia was showing just how little sense that makes. You always have to change to stay well and ahead of the game.

Me: You see, Rodrigo, change is good! There's no reason to be afraid of it.

Julia: Let's go over the reasons preventing you from starting a career in gastronomy.

She took a pen from her purse and, in perfect elementary school teacher handwriting, wrote a list of reasons on a paper napkin based on the points that Rodrigo had made:

1. Passion and work don't mix.

2. Don't trade a sure thing for something uncertain.

3. Risking everything without being prepared is crazy.

With these points noted, we sought counterarguments to convince Rodrigo to change.

Me: Let's go through it point by point. The first one is total nonsense. Work and passion can mix. And when that happens, it's great! It's like love and sex!

I noticed that the comment embarrassed Julia a little. I thought it best to return to the topic of work.

Me: I love my new job and even got a promotion.

Julia: I'm also passionate about my work. I don't see why anyone shouldn't like what they do.

Interesting, the way Julia said it. She didn't say "do what they like," but "like what they do." There's no reason to be unhappy and live a miserable life in any job. If Rodrigo decided to continue working in the Call Center, he would have to learn to enjoy and be motivated by his job. I changed that in my last days at the Call Center, when I started orienting myself toward outcomes, and I was very motivated. On the other hand, if he changed jobs to cooking but dedicated himself only to completing tasks in the kitchen of a restaurant and delivering outputs without motivation for a delicious dish, eventually he would have a job as sad as the current one. The orientation to outcomes is what generates a feeling of purpose and motivation.

> Me: Working with passion is essential for a happy life. Cross out that first item.

Julia crossed out the first item, and we moved on to the second: "Don't trade a sure thing for something uncertain."

> Julia: That doesn't seem to be a universal truth either. If, at a crossroads, there are two signs, one saying, "This way there is only suffering and pain," and the other saying, "This way there is a chance of happiness," anyone would opt for the second. Some chance is better than none.

> Me: That's true. If you're unhappy where you are and don't have the chance to improve, swapping the certain for the uncertain makes sense and might even be recommended. You also have to consider that what might seem certain may not be. Just because you're employed in the Call Center today doesn't mean it's a guaranteed job. The scenario can change, and the bank can fire you anytime. Who knows? A job doesn't guarantee anything.

I didn't want to go into detail and reveal what Oscar had told me about the bank being at risk from competitors. It also seemed unlikely that the Call Center would close and everyone would be fired, but you can't be sure. In addition to the bank's competitors, there was the risk that new technologies would replace the type of service that Rodrigo did. Or the bank could decide to outsource the service, as several other companies have already done. Anything can change at any time. There's no certainty in any job. The only two certainties we have in life are that one day we'll die and that, until then, we'll go through numerous changes.

Julia crossed out the second item, and we moved on to the third: "Risking everything without being prepared is crazy." This item made me pause. I was doing that on my journey to try to understand and transform the bank's culture and make it more innovative, and I wondered if I wasn't the one who was a few sandwiches short of a picnic. I was taking a substantial risk. Just as Rodrigo was preparing himself with the Asian cooking course and Julia wanted to take a therapeutic follow-up course, I should probably have been looking for some training to carry out my role in the Innovation Department with a more technical foundation.

> Me: Let's think about a risk minimization strategy so you don't have to risk everything. It's not like you have to quit your job at the bank tomorrow, rent a huge space, and set up a restaurant the next day. That would be too risky, for sure! Why don't you start a small business as an experiment and gradually learn and accumulate experience? Without quitting the bank. Something you do in your spare time.

> Julia: How about making some delicacies and frozen dishes to sell to friends and acquaintances? Surely

your colleagues at the bank would be interested, and you'd be able to find out what sells the most and gives the best results.

Rodrigo's expression began to change as we tried to convince him. Our arguments made sense, and he seemed to be warming up to the idea.

Rodrigo: It would also be possible to test what I like doing best and if I can mix work with pleasure.

Me: That's right. You can have dinners like the one you made for us today, inviting more people and charging them for the experience.

Julia: I think this list of fears deserves special treatment. It's time for your life to transcend and take on a new flavor, like your Zen Garden of white fish sashimi.

Julia closed her left hand and, little by little, pushed the napkin into her closed fist, squeezing it with her fingers until there was only a small piece of paper poking out and then nothing. When the whole napkin was hidden inside her hand, she blew hard and magically opened both hands. The napkin was gone.

Rodrigo: Wow! That tops my magic sauce!

We clapped, and I was amused to see that the box of tricks from China was already in action. I knew it would be a big hit with the kids, but I didn't expect such a scene during dinner. It was witty and masterfully timed. The girl has talent!

Me: Seriously, Rodrigo, I'd be willing to pay to eat the delicious things you made today. You can count on me as a customer.

Julia: Me too. I don't have much money, but I would save up to come at least once in a while to taste these treats.

Rodrigo: If that's the case, you can start paying today! The dirty dishes are all yours.

Me: It's a steal!

We laughed, took out the dishes, and went to the kitchen to clean up. Julia washed up, and I rinsed and dried. Rodrigo was thoughtful, plucking up the courage to take the first steps that could bring about a revolution in his life.

In the political sense, a revolution is a movement of revolt against an established power. It aims to promote profound changes in political, economic, cultural, and moral institutions.

I reflected that the changes needed at the bank fit this definition. Established power isn't necessarily a government or a person. It can be a set of ideas, values, and biases that guide behaviors. Changing your mindset is a revolution. It takes courage to be a revolutionary.

> *Change, for when we change, the world changes with us*
> *We change the world in the changing of the mind*
> *And when the mind changes, we move forward.*[5]

---

5. "Até quando?" (Until when?), a song by the Brazilian writer and rapper Gabriel o Pensador (Gabriel the Thinker), known for his awareness-raising lyrics. He explores activism and topics like racism, politics, and religion.

Chapter 23: The Bad One and the Good One

On Monday, I met with Oscar first thing in the morning. I had scheduled a meeting with him to present the results of my surveys and diagnoses on the state bank's corporate culture, stating how I would classify its current (output-driven) state and what the desired (outcome-driven) state would look like. I simplified my presentation as much as possible so the main ideas could be shared with anyone simply and were quickly understood using the concept of mindset.

I was confident about the diagnosis but didn't yet know what treatment would change the culture. The conversations with the managers and their rejection, when I tried to share this information, intimidated me a little. I felt like a doctor who has diagnosed a patient with diabetes, but the patient doesn't want to stop eating sweets. I hoped Oscar could come up with a solution for this.

Oscar: Welcome. I'm looking forward to seeing the results of your work.

Me: To map the corporate culture, I used the concepts of output and outcome that you taught me and the mindset concept that I learned from Barbara. I hope you like how it turned out.

I explained to Oscar that I was using the term "mindset" to represent the predisposition of each person to think, feel, and act the way they normally think, feel, and act. If this pattern is repeated within an organization, the collective mindset is called corporate culture.

As he had already noted, our current corporate culture was output-driven. Our employees worked toward delivering the tasks assigned to them. They lacked commitment to outcomes and a broader view of their role within a more complex ecosystem. These failures led to rework and waste, making the company slow to identify opportunities for improvement and unable to take the necessary corrective actions promptly.

I presented the table below, which summarizes the differences between output-driven and outcome-driven mindsets in all their aspects: the invisible part (thinking and feeling) and the visible part (acting).

I had already partially presented this result, but now we had the whole mindset mapped out in a way that could explain why things happened the way they did. To change behavior, we would have to modify beliefs and values and transform how people feel in the organization.

	Output-Driven Mindset	Outcome-Driven Mindset
THINK	**Limited** I worry about my own success.	**Holistic** I understand value for everyone.
	Compliant I am responsible for doing things right.	**Effective** I am responsible for making sure the right things get done.
FEEL	**Averse to Debate** I have no patience for differing opinions.	**Open to Listening** I am sensitive to different personalities and their unique needs.
	Fearful I feel uncomfortable when there is ambiguity or uncertainty.	**Bold** I love learning new things. Challenges motivate me.
ACT	**Rigid** I resist change and avoid new ideas.	**Adaptable** I always challenge the status quo.
	Obedient I follow explicit instructions without question.	**Creative** I figure out how to achieve the best result.
	Individualistic I ignore other points of view.	**Collaborative** I take responsibility for collaboration and shared understanding.

Oscar was silent for a few seconds, looking at the table and reflecting. Then he nodded his head and said:

Oscar: This is looking really good! In a few words and an easy-to-understand model, you have captured the essence of the cultural transformation we need to make. The outcome-driven mindset is exactly what this organization needs to innovate. It's a way for us to continually sense and respond to market changes. Congratulations! This model is much more than I had expected.

I swelled with pride. What a satisfying moment. Anyone who looked superficially at this table would think it's no big deal. They wouldn't imagine all the interviews and stories behind the conclusions presented here in a simple framework. But Oscar was aware of my work and could clearly see the importance of it. He was the one who had set and was now guiding me on this journey. The fruits of my labor were his as well. And we were both delighted to have found a way to sum it up so neatly.

But would that be enough to change the organization's culture?

Me: In the first round of interviews, I discovered two problems—the unnecessary restriction of loan collateral by The Rule of Three and the misalignment between the Marketing and Operations departments in the launch of extended intelligence. Those involved promptly set out to promote changes and correct the situation. Just identifying the problem was enough.

Oscar: And those involved were grateful for your input when the issues were brought to light.

Me: Yes. It was very rewarding. However, the behavior was very different during the interviews with the managers. I identified several problems created by an output-driven mindset that needed to be solved, but they didn't seem willing to change. I faced enormous resistance when I tried to talk to them about the problems.

Oscar: What needs to change?

Me: A lot! You need to modify the Call Center's indicators and rewards policy. Several systems need to be integrated to optimize the workflow. Accounting for payments needs to be redesigned from end to end. We also need to review the archive retention policy to identify what records are truly valuable and discard the rest. That's just for starters. I can't see the whole picture yet!

Oscar: The output and outcome-driven mindset chart you've made is a beautiful map that shows the starting point and direction for cultural change, but it's not enough to have a map in hand. You have to take the path. And this path must be followed by the people working in this culture. They're the ones who need to be transformed.

Me: They won't be able to do that on their own. Someone needs to lead them through this process of organizational transformation.

Oscar: And that will be your new role. You're the one who will lead the transformation not only of the processes, systems, indicators, and policies you have commented on but, more importantly, of the mindset of all those involved in these changes. As an enabler of organizational transformation, you'll be an agent of corporate culture change for innovation.

Rodrigo's voice echoed from a distant corner of my memory, like when the hero of a story remembers a curse cast on him many chapters ago: *Any initiative will be severely punished!* It seemed as though my punishment would be to solve each of the problems I had identified.

I was terrified. I didn't have the experience like Barbara to lead a group in a meeting and bring everyone to a consensus. I didn't even know the techniques for modeling and mapping and what was needed to transform the organization. I was not prepared for the task.

But at the same time, I felt an immense desire to learn. This would be an organizational transformation that would generate great value for the bank and being the facilitator responsible for it was a great professional and learning opportunity for me. I realized that whether I looked at this work as "punishment" or "reward" depended on my mindset. This was my chance to apply the mindset transformation model and direct myself toward outcomes. This thought motivated me to accept the challenge.

Me: You can count on me. It will be a privilege.

It's not that I wasn't afraid of the challenge—the fear was still there. I realized that courage has nothing to do with not being afraid. Those who aren't afraid in the face of danger or the unknown aren't courageous. They're probably just misinformed or naïve. Courage is doing something despite being afraid.

> Me: I think I'll need help with that. I don't have the necessary experience, but I thought I'd get some recommendations from Barbara. What do you think?

> Oscar: That's an excellent idea. She's the best person to be your mentor in this new role. I'll tell her you'll be in touch.

Chapter 24: Welcome to Business Analysis

When I arrived, Barbara was at her desk answering messages on the computer. She didn't have her own office or anything like that—just a desk in a cubicle in the middle of the IT Systems Development Department. Several other analysts were working at their desks in the same space, separated only by small partitions about four feet high. Some were talking loudly on the phone, others between themselves. It was a busy, noisy environment with zero privacy, not unlike the Call Center.

On her desk were several books and paper documents. Next to the computer, there was a photo of Barbara and a man. Their arms were around each other as they stood in front of the Eiffel Tower. I assumed it was her husband.

Barbara: Pull up that chair and sit down so we can talk.

Me: Thanks. I've never been to Paris. Is it as beautiful as they say?

Barbara: It's packed with tourists—well, it is the most visited city in the world, but it doesn't lose its charm. Paris is beautiful! My husband and I took a trip there about five years ago, and it was absolutely wonderful. The Louvre is sensational. The Arc de Triomphe, the Champs-Élysées, Montmartre... it's well worth a visit! I love to travel and learn about different places and things. What about you?

Me: I'm still learning to enjoy learning. Seeing a trip as a learning opportunity is kind of strange to me. My vacations have always been dedicated to rest and relaxation—beach and chill. I have always related learning to school and obligation, so savoring learning is a mindset shift that I'm still working on.

Barbara smiled as she realized I was doing self-analysis for personal development. The examples set by Rodrigo and Julia had made me reflect on how I dealt with my own learning. I still didn't know what or how, but I was convinced I needed to invest more in my education.

Barbara: You're on the right track. You'll discover many things you like and fall deeper in love as you learn more about them.

Me: I hope I can learn how to do what you did in that workshop I attended on the leads system for Marketing. The way you conducted the meeting and helped all the participants express themselves and reach a consensus was inspiring!

Barbara: Thank you. What I did there and what I practice

every day in my work is called business analysis. I think that's what you're looking for.

Me: You think so? I don't know. I'm not an IT person. My place is in the Innovation Department with Oscar.

Barbara: Here at the State Bank, business analyst is only a formal position within IT. But business analysis isn't limited to technology. That's because it focuses on understanding business much more broadly. Many other professionals who don't work as business analysts also "do" business analysis, such as project managers, enterprise architects, business managers, and consultants. It's a learning experience that can benefit anyone.

Me: I'm not sure I understand what business analysis is.

Barbara: Business analysis is the practice of enabling change in the context of an enterprise by defining needs and recommending solutions that deliver the most value to stakeholders.

I felt like that definition related to what I had been doing. I had spent days trying to identify needs in the company from a holistic point of view. Now, I needed to find the solution to generate the most value in each context and promote organizational change.

Me: I like this definition. Did you come up with that definition yourself?

Barbara: No. This definition is part of the standard

defined by an international association[6] that maps concepts and techniques to help us do our job.

I lacked knowledge and mastery of these techniques that business analysts use daily to do their jobs more effectively.

I briefly told Barbara about my journey, which involved going through various departments and conducting interviews until I formulated the summary framework for the change of mindset.

> Barbara: I see that you've already used some classic business analysis techniques. Interviews, observation, and document analysis are techniques for eliciting information.
>
> Me: Eliciting?
>
> Barbara: Eliciting is bringing out something that's hidden. Some use the term "collect" or "gather" information, but I prefer the word "elicit" because it emphasizes the need to dive deep and discover things that aren't visible. It's a lot of work, and you need to be a bit of a detective.

I felt exactly like a kind of Sherlock Holmes, uncovering clues and unraveling mysteries. I hadn't realized that I was doing business analysis while talking to people, but when I thought about it, I was doing just that: analyzing the business to identify opportunities for improvement.

---

6. The International Institute of Business Analysis (IIBA) supports the recognition of business analysis within organizations. It enables networking and community engagement, provides foundational standards and resources, and offers internationally recognized certification programs for career advancement.

Barbara: There are many other techniques that you can learn and apply to your work.

Amid the pile of books on her desk, Barbara picked up a hefty orange volume titled *A Guide to the Business Analysis Body of Knowledge (BABOK Guide)*. I was startled by its thickness—it was over 500 pages long.

Me: It looks like a Bible!

She laughed.

Barbara: I got my certification as a business analysis professional over a decade ago and highly recommend it to any professional. The process of preparing for an exam encourages us to develop and learn.

Once again, my mindset was being put to the test. I never liked studying. I had always looked at learning as an imposition. After leaving school, I felt tremendously relieved that I'd never have to take another test again. At that moment, Barbara was inviting me on a learning journey with an immense volume that wasn't even a textbook. She said it was just a guide to everything I would need to learn to pass an exam. That meant that besides the 500-page guide, I would have to look for additional content to learn things. And she thought this would be stimulating. My first reaction was, "Are you kidding me?"

Me: There's so much to learn. I don't have time to study.

Barbara laughed.

Barbara: Studying is the fastest way to learn. Only someone with a lot of spare time can afford to learn by trial and error. If you want to learn quickly, you'd better take advantage of the knowledge of people who have already made many mistakes and have organized the knowledge they've gained. That way, you can learn without going through all the suffering they've been through.

I thought again of the dinner prepared by Rodrigo and how happy he seemed to learn new cooking methods. I remembered Julia's motivation to become a therapeutic companion and work in an entirely new field. A similar opportunity was coming my way and I needed to change my mindset again.

Me: Okay. Where do I start?

Barbara: You must learn to enjoy learning. It can take a while, but it's worth it. The key is to choose a subject that interests you and fall in love with it. Take it step by step, starting with easier challenges and then increasing the difficulty, like in a video game. With each level of the game, you become more skilled and feel rewarded. A certification exam encourages you to study specific content and can serve as a milestone of success. More straightforward things like finishing a book or taking an online course are also good ways to get started. Everyone should find a topic and learning strategy that suits them best, but the point is to never stop learning.

This conversation was a turning point for me. I would need to learn a lot of new things to move forward, but this wasn't necessarily a bad thing. On the contrary, I discovered that constant learning is one of the secrets of happiness.

Chapter 25: The Emperor's New Clothes

Changing other people's mindsets is quite a different thing from changing one's own. What made me become outcome-driven was internal discomfort with my status quo. I was frustrated, uninspired, and despondent. And as strange as it may seem, I felt more inspired when I generated value not only for myself but for others. Helping Oscar access his mother's account that day was a victory. It was immensely satisfying to find opportunities for improvements at the State Bank, like unmasking the Rule of Three, realigning investments in the extended intelligence service system, and reviewing the flow of the purple folders. I knew I wouldn't personally benefit from any of these improvements, but a lot of other people would. That alone gave me a huge burst of energy to make it happen. The question is, can this mindset be implemented from the outside into other people's thoughts, feelings, and behaviors? Could I really transform corporate culture as Oscar would like me to?

Hand still on her keyboard, Barbara answered my question

with a level gaze.

Barbara: Business analysis is the key to this transformation. There's nothing more inspiring than a purpose. Business analysis gives us exactly that by aligning an organization's activities with its strategic purpose.

Me: Then why do so many people get stuck in an output-driven mindset?

Barbara: I don't think it's a conscious choice. People often don't understand the importance of their work as part of the whole. They become alienated.

Me: You mean they can't see what difference they make?

Barbara: Exactly. When people realize they're not insignificant, they identify opportunities to generate better results. Action and inspiration create cycles of feedback that lead to a change in mindset. Change is a process.

Me: So I need to stop thinking of an outcome-driven mindset as a destination and think of it as a journey. Are you saying what I need to do is set the ball rolling?

Barbara's eyes smiled, and she gave the tiniest nod. Then I remembered the list of managers, and my returning smile died on my lips. Set the ball rolling? Trying to push a massive boulder uphill was a more accurate description.

Me: There are some pretty tough nuts to crack.

Barbara: A perfect place to start.

We decided to test our hypothesis with the managers I thought were lost causes. Oscar helped get the other directors on board. We scheduled a one-day workshop with Mr. Andrade, my former Call Center manager, and another with Adelaide, who's responsible for the purple folders in Accounting, to discuss possible improvements in their departments as identified in my survey.

I wasn't particularly optimistic. I was more likely to convince a cat to take a bath than get these two to change their mindset. I prepared myself to leave the workshop disappointed (and defeated), but Barbara was quick to call me out on my attitude:

> Barbara: If you go into a game to lose, that's exactly what will happen.
>
> Me: Well, I have to be realistic in my expectations.
>
> Barbara: Be careful about what you choose to expect. It's very likely what you'll get. Have a little faith. Trust the technique. You've seen for yourself that business analysis, if properly conducted, helps create a clearer vision of what's happening. People see the existing problems, how they can help, and work together for better solutions. Everything will turn out fine.

I got the message. If adopting a mindset is a conscious decision, it was time to make my own. I was the one orchestrating this change, so the first one to be bold and motivated by the challenge was me. And I would need to be adaptable to challenge the status quo of our corporate culture. Bold and adaptable. Two characteristics of the outcome-driven mindset. I got the feeling the managers weren't the only ones who would be learning from this workshop.

The first workshop was aimed at the Call Center customer service. Mr. Andrade brought one of the attendants to add to the discussion. I was surprised to see my former, very much output-driven, colleague.

> Me: Rodrigo! Great to have your input!

> Rodrigo: I heard the coffee machine is better than the one at the Call Center, so I came to check it out. Now, that would be a major improvement—changing the coffee machine—huh?

> Me: It would indeed! Unfortunately, the coffee machine is not on the agenda.

> Rodrigo: Who knows, maybe it was the bad coffee that caused you to spend so long in the restroom that time!

> Me: Shhh!

He was joking, but his thinking was typical of someone who can't see beyond improvements for personal benefit. There was nothing to motivate him to achieve a higher purpose.

Mr. Andrade was curious about what the workshop would entail, but he politely held back his questions. Barbara was, as always, extremely personable and immediately tuned in to everyone she was talking to. "Rapport personified," I thought.

The friendly atmosphere warmed up even more as we cut into a delicious corncake, courtesy of Rodrigo. Of course, I knew it was a sneaky free sample, and several orders quickly followed. At least he was starting to take his food business more seriously.

> Barbara: This workshop was designed to identify opportunities for improving how your department thinks, feels, and works. I ask that you be open to questioning some of your assumptions and participate as openly as possible. It will be a collaborative process, and we will create everything as a group.

> Mr. Andrade: Of course. However, as you know, our department is a reference in service quality. Our indicators are well above the market average, and we maintain a team highly dedicated to meeting our goals. I'm curious to see what else we can improve on.

Oh my God! Where did this man get the idea that dropping calls to keep the service time on target was synonymous with quality? I kept my expression neutral and my mouth shut. It wasn't the time. He would have to work it out for himself.

Barbara introduced us to stakeholder analysis as the first business analysis technique. We brainstormed all the people or groups who had some relationship with the work in the Call Center. Then, we rated each of them on their degree of influence and impact and placed them in a 2x2 matrix.

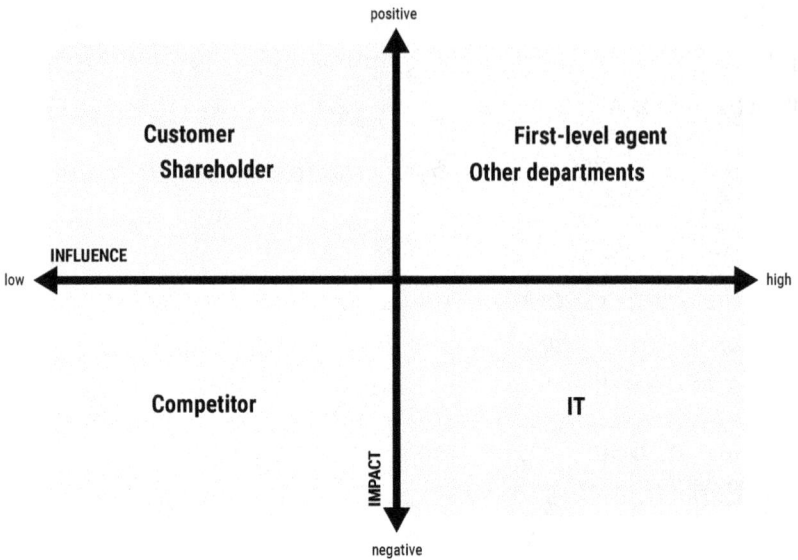

```
                              positive
                                 ▲
                                 |
         Customer                |      First-level agent
        Shareholder              |      Other departments
                                 |
  INFLUENCE                      |
  low ◄────────────────────────────────────────────► high
                                 |
         Competitor              |           IT
                                 |
                            IMPACT▼
                              negative
```

According to this technique:

- **Influence** is related to a stakeholder's power. An influential stakeholder has the authority to add or remove resources from an initiative.

- **Impact** measures the stakeholder's interest in possible changes. In some cases, the impact of a change may harm, threaten, or bring negative consequences to a stakeholder.

With stakeholders classified into four quadrants, we mapped out the most appropriate strategies to deal with each.

In the first quadrant were the customers who consume the bank's services and the shareholders who receive the profits. All of these need to be protected. This means that any change we make to the Call Center must consider their interests first. It's up to us to guarantee a positive impact for them.

Rodrigo: Aren't shareholders highly influential?

Barbara: They can be influential in other contexts, but not here. The impact on them should be positive. After all, the company exists to provide services to customers and profit to the shareholders, but they don't participate in our decisions to optimize the Call Center. So we can't really say they have power. Rather, it's our responsibility to ensure their needs are understood and met.

Improvements in the Call Center tend to negatively impact competitors, but as they have little influence, we can ignore them.

Forming a partnership is the best approach for stakeholders with high influence and a positive impact, such as first-level attendants who carry out the work, represented here by Rodrigo, and other departments that provide second-level service. They all share the same goal of meeting customer needs.

IT appeared in the quadrant that Barbara called "the riskiest." They have a high influence because the service is dependent on the systems developed and maintained by IT. However, their objectives differ, and they may not prioritize the Call Center needs among many other demands. If we depend on them, we need to earn their partnership by finding opportunities to meet their needs in return.

From my point of view, it was already clear that the Call Center had its priorities all wrong. Like someone who spends a fortune on clothes and jewelry to impress others but can't pay their electricity bill. Mr. Andrade's goals and practices produced enviable indicators within the industry,

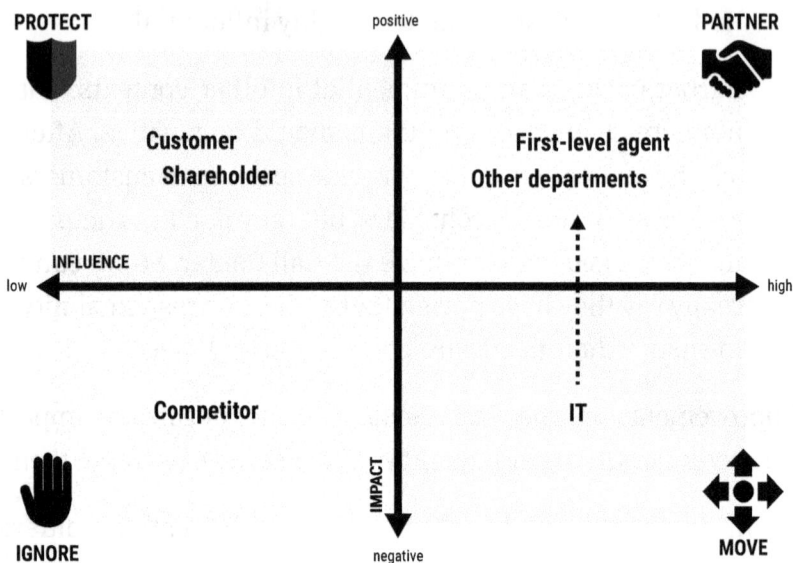

PROTECT

positive

PARTNER

Customer
Shareholder

First-level agent
Other departments

INFLUENCE

low ← → high

Competitor

IT

IMPACT

negative

IGNORE

MOVE

but they did little to meet customer needs and maximize gains for shareholders.

As unmistakable as it was to me, the problem was still far from obvious to Mr. Andrade. But things soon changed when Barbara presented our company's Vision Statement.

STATE BANK VISION

To be recognized as the most innovative retail bank, leading the transformation of the financial sector to empower our customers and community with excellence in customer service and ethical and sustainable banking practices.

Barbara: Everything we do in the company—our processes, decisions, investments, and performance indicators—must align with the strategic north represented in our vision. Let's construct a more localized vision of the ideals and values of Call Center customer service that's still in keeping with the bank's vision.

It was our collaborative task to create a statement not identical to the bank's vision statement but derived from it. We were looking for qualifiers to guide customer service in the Call Center. We all put in our two cents, adding or changing a word until we arrived at this result.

> Barbara: Now, looking at this vision statement, can you see any opportunities for improvement in how the Call Center runs?

CALL CENTER VISION	QUALIFIERS
To be the benchmark in customer service in the banking industry, excelling through innovation, personalization, and the ability to respond quickly to the needs of our customers, setting standards of excellence and trust.	• agility • empathy • innovation • customization • effectiveness • excellence • trust

> Rodrigo: Empathy and trust. We don't really put ourselves in the customer's shoes. For me, serving customers is just another task.

Rodrigo said this with a mixture of misgiving and relief. It was a bit like saying, "The Emperor has no clothes!" Everyone knew it, but no one dared to speak out. If truth be told, the emperor's birthday suit had been on display for quite some time, but the impressive indicators and departmental prestige loomed over the Call Center employees. It required more courage than most mortals possessed to disagree with how things run. Now, though, focusing on stakeholders and the vision statement, it was difficult *not* to disagree.

As someone who had worked in the Call Center, I knew precisely what Rodrigo meant. Mr. Andrade's policy of dropping calls after a specific time meant the AHT (Average Holding Time) was low, and the Call Center presented enviable numbers compared to industry benchmarks. However, it generated significant dissatisfaction from customers whose problems weren't solved.

Mr. Andrade was clearly ill at ease, but he didn't conceal or contradict Rodrigo's claim. The precise definition of the strategic vision had brought him a sudden and disturbing realization–the practices of his department in no way reflected the statement he had just helped write.

> Mr. Andrade: In the Call Center, we guide our practices using indicators we didn't choose and never question. Considering our vision statement, they don't seem to be a good fit for the company. Is there any way we can change these drivers to improve results?

It's hard to describe how I felt when I heard Mr. Andrade say that. Imagine a father who spends the whole morning balancing his son on a bike and then, at the magic moment, sees him pedal off on his own. It was like that.

Barbara: Of course we can. That's exactly why we're here—to identify opportunities for better outcomes. The way we assess people directly influences their behavior, so indicators and targets are significant influencers of corporate culture. If they aren't aligned with the strategy, the indicators can cause considerable damage. What changes do you suggest?

Mr. Andrade scratched his chin and closed his eyes for a moment. Judging from his expression, a quiet revolution was taking place in a mind that was always directed by the established goals, never questioning—and never seeing the bigger picture.

Mr. Andrade: It's clear that the customer's perspective is key. If we're to protect our customers and guarantee their satisfaction, our indicator should measure the average time to respond to the customer's need. The clock can only stop when the customer confirms that their need has been met.

Me: What if multiple calls are required to resolve the customer's needs?

Mr. Andrade: Too bad. We have to count from when the need was identified to when it was met. Even if it takes days. We won't end up with such pretty numbers, but it doesn't matter. We'll be focused on reducing response time from the customer's perspective.

Barbara: I think it's a great idea. We're moving in the right direction by looking at the perspective of the customer who is having their need met. Along the same lines, we could have an indicator that evaluates the average number of calls a customer needs to make.

This was a major shift that would change the entire focus of customer service. The clock keeps running until the customer confirms their need has been answered.

Rodrigo: I don't think our customer service system is capable of identifying whether the customer's need was met. There's no distinction between call and service.

We used a technique called concept modeling to differentiate the terms and structure the concepts necessary to define these indicators clearly so that they could be implemented and monitored in automated systems.

From these definitions, we expressed clearly that a customer can make multiple calls until a need is resolved. It was also

Concept Model Diagram

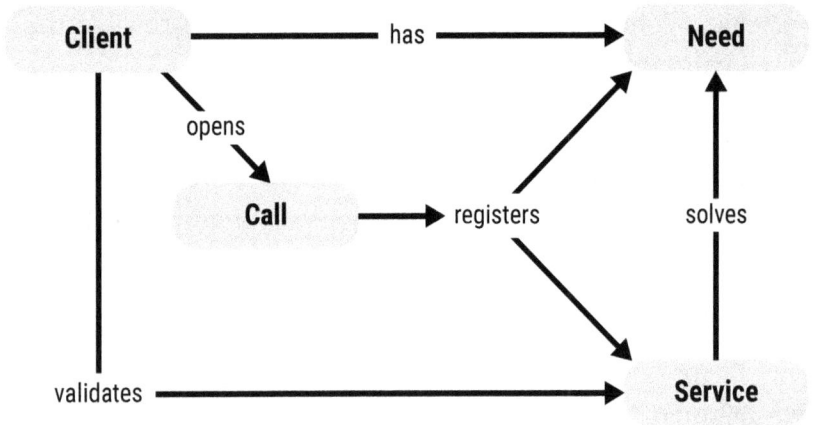

Glossary of Terms

Term	Definition	Examples
Need	A customer requirement issue that the bank can resolve.	Access to specific information, a configuration, or a new copy of a card.
Service	A set of activities the bank carries out to resolve a customer's need.	A change of the customer's address in the bank's systems.
Call	A communication the customer makes to the bank's Call Center to resolve a need.	John Smith's call on a Wednesday to request a second copy of a card.

clear that only the customer could validate the service received and evaluate how their need was resolved, supporting a new indicator of client satisfaction.

Several policy and system changes would be necessary to optimize the process with these new indicators. We discussed and mapped some of them, including automation between systems, greater autonomy for first-level agents, and new monitoring panels. I was so involved in the analysis that I almost forgot that the objective behind this workshop was to validate whether business analysis techniques could bring about a change in mindset. That's when I heard the phrase that made my day.

Mr. Andrade: Thank you for looking at the Call Center with us and contributing to the identification of so many opportunities for innovation. I feel more excited than I have in a long time. I know there's a lot of work to be done, but I'm looking forward to implementing these changes.

My jaw dropped. I looked at Barbara. She winked back as if to say, "See?" Countless times, she had witnessed what happens when people have the opportunity to see their business more clearly. Mr. Andrade had always been committed to his work; he just didn't have the right information. With his new outcome-driven perspective, he was ready to make sure the right things got done in his department.

I felt a familiar rush of excitement. I couldn't wait to tell Oscar about the success of the workshop. I was already imagining what the outcome would be like with Adelaide and the purple folders. Rodrigo and Mr. Andrade departed, and as we left the meeting room, Barbara hit me with some unexpected news.

Barbara: I'm afraid I won't be able to participate in the workshop with Accounting and Finance. But I'm confident you'll do an excellent job as the facilitator.

Chapter 26: Dominoes

Tapestries, candles, banners, and royal coats of arms jostled for attention as Westminster Abbey heaved with the elaborately dressed presence of the entire court. The youth at the center of all eyes holds his posture stiffly as he swears the sacred oath and is anointed with the holy oil of divine choice. Sweat runs down a forehead he cannot touch as the Archbishop of Canterbury raises the crown of England's sovereign above his head. It is the supreme moment. Every breath is held when a beggar with the exact same countenance as the prince bursts through the abbey's main door.

Stop at once! This man is an impostor.

When Mark Twain tells us that the Prince of Wales exchanges position with an abused and lowly beggar, we know it can't end that way. The identical appearance of the disadvantaged double might fool the court initially, but the impostor will inevitably be revealed.

That scene replayed in my head as I contemplated the second mindset transformation workshop. I wasn't an experienced business analyst like Barbara. I wasn't sure my own outcome-driven mindset was even completely consolidated. It was all very uncertain, and yet it was my responsibility to ensure everyone could understand the problems of the purple folder flow.

Adelaide was impatient. She was upset about attending anything that would take up her precious time. On the previous day, the branches had made municipal tax payments, and she liked to check the entries personally to make sure nothing had been left out of the purple folder. The deadline wouldn't wait, and she would have to work overtime to make up for the time spent in the workshop.

> Adelaide: Is my presence really necessary?

I confirmed that it was. Adelaide blinked hard and fiddled with her glasses in annoyance.

Also participating were Andrew, the analyst from the Finance Department with whom I had spoken previously, and Oswald, the specialist from the Legal Department.

Mindful of Barbara's incredible people skills, I did everything to repeat the success of the previous workshop, even down to ordering a corn cake to share with the participants before we started.

> Adelaide: Thank you, but I'm on a diet. I can't eat sugar or gluten.

And the ball's gone wide of the goal! At least my efforts weren't lost on the others.

Oswald: Wow! This cake is delicious.

Andrew: Fantastic. Where did you buy it?

While Rodrigo picked up more customers, the deliciousness of the cake irritated Adelaide even more.

Adelaide: Can we get to the point?

A beggar pretending to be a prince, I stepped into Barbara's shoes as the facilitator.

Me: This workshop is designed to identify opportunities for improvement. I ask you to be open to questioning the way things currently happen and to feel comfortable expressing your thoughts. We'll decide everything in consensus.

Oswald: Consensus is somewhat of a utopia. We're from different departments and see the company in quite different ways. This may take quite some time.

That was all I needed—friendly fire from Oswald, the one person I considered an ally in the workshop! I thought Adelaide would explode when she heard his comment. I quickly responded that business analysis techniques would help us build a shared vision of the whole and asked for a vote of confidence to move forward. In truth, though, Oscar and the directors had summoned the participants, and none of them had any choice.

Adelaide: Fine. Let's save some time, then. I have here the sequence of activities of the flow of the purple folders. Our department is already well structured.

She produced a view of the process restricted to what happens within Accounting. It didn't consider the flow passing through different areas of the organization, from payment to data storage.

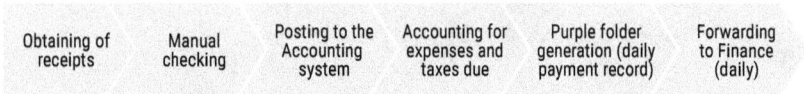

Obtaining of receipts	Manual checking	Posting to the Accounting system	Accounting for expenses and taxes due	Purple folder generation (daily payment record)	Forwarding to Finance (daily)

Me: Okay. Now, let's consider that this business process starts before the Accounting Department obtains the receipts and ends after they're forwarded to the Finance Department. Accounting is just one of several actors participating in a more extensive process related to supplier payments. Let's have a look at payments from start to finish.

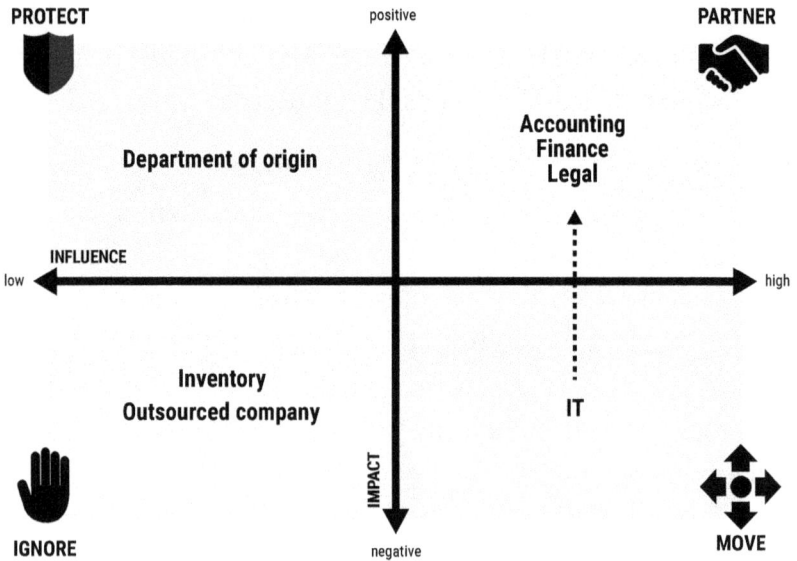

PROTECT — positive — PARTNER

Department of origin

Accounting Finance Legal

INFLUENCE — low ← → high

Inventory Outsourced company — IT

IMPACT

IGNORE — negative — MOVE

Following in Barbara's footsteps, I started with a stakeholder analysis. With everyone's help, we identified everyone involved in or impacted by the process related to the purple folders and placed them in an influence vs. impact matrix.

Getting to this point wasn't easy. None of the participants had a clear vision beyond their department or were aware of all the stakeholders. I found it interesting that although IT was in the same place as in the previous workshop, all the other stakeholders differed. The role of each person in this process was unclear.

> Andrew: Now I know what you mean by end-to-end flow. We're used to seeing the process only within our department as if it were a complete process, but it's part of a broader whole that passes through several areas.

> Adelaide: The important thing is that everyone performs their part of the work with excellence. We're all part of a big engine, and I can assure you that the Accounting gear is working perfectly. If I have to manage the work of other departments as well, I'll need more than 24 hours in a day to get everything done.

Adelaide was impatient and made it obvious she thought the workshop was a waste of time. We were holding up her day.

Oswald said nothing. He pursed his lips and looked at me over his glasses with an expression that translated into "I told you so."

I glanced longingly at the door and imagined Barbara rushing into the room to rescue me, dressed in the clothes of the old lady in front of the post office with the toy guitar and shouting, "Stop at once! This man is an impostor!" But there was no one there. The workshop depended on me, and it was time to let life take me.

> Me: I think it's important to consider the bigger picture to optimize the parts. What do you think, Oswald?

Seeing my despair, the specialist came to my aid with a far more informed and erudite speech than I could ever have made.

> Oswald: The mechanistic metaphor can be helpful in limited contexts, but it's inadequate for describing complexity. An organic or systemic metaphor would be more suitable for understanding how interconnected parts evolve.

What he said was perfect. I don't know if the others really got it, though. Andrew was looking at the floor as if he had dropped something while Oswald was speaking. Adelaide remained unwavering in her disdain.

> Me: Let me see if I understand. You're saying that a company is more like an organism than a machine. So, for example, if I have high blood pressure, there's no point in just examining my heart. I need to see myself as a whole and understand my diet, whether I exercise, and whether my other organs are fulfilling their role. Is that it?

> Oswald: Exactly.

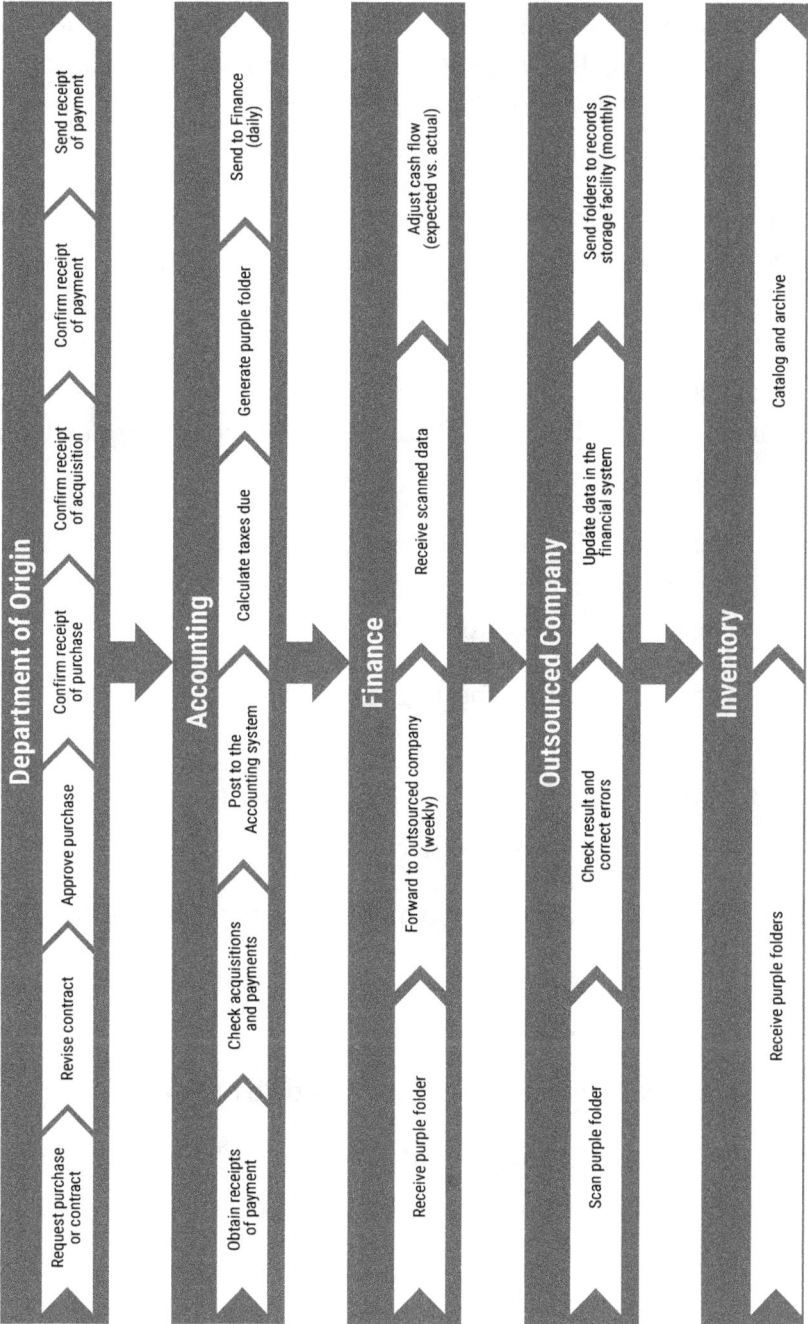

Department of Origin

Request purchase or contract → Revise contract → Approve purchase → Confirm receipt of purchase → Confirm receipt of acquisition → Confirm receipt of payment → Send receipt of payment

Accounting

Obtain receipts of payment → Check acquisitions and payments → Post to the Accounting system → Calculate taxes due → Generate purple folder → Send to Finance (daily)

Finance

Receive purple folder → Forward to outsourced company (weekly) → Receive scanned data → Adjust cash flow (expected vs. actual)

Outsourced Company

Scan purple folder → Check result and correct errors → Update data in the financial system → Send folders to records storage facility (monthly)

Inventory

Receive purple folders → Catalog and archive

Me: Okay. Let's apply that. Based on my surveys, I have prepared a diagram of the flow of purple folders passing through different departments. I would like you to evaluate it and tell me what you think.

Barbara had helped me put together this diagram, and I was waiting for the right moment to present it. It was the ace up my sleeve to ensure that those involved could have a holistic view. As they read the picture, they asked questions and confirmed that this was exactly what was happening. It was the first time that Adelaide had seen the whole process, and some questions finally began to emerge.

Adelaide: Why does the outsourced company need to check the purple folders if we've already checked everything in Accounting?

Andrew: Because the scanning process can generate errors in the purple folder data.

Adelaide: The scanning process?! Why are you having the purple folders scanned?

Andrew: Because it's too much work to scan internally.

Adelaide: But why do they need to be scanned? We could just send you the file with the data.

Andrew: The file...? You have this data on file?

Adelaide: Of course we do! We need all the data in a database to be able to print the purple folder.

Andrew: Are you serious? And no one ever noticed?! Good grief. We don't even need the purple folders!

Adelaide: But the purple folder goes to the records storage facility to be cataloged and archived. There must be some legal requirement to retain physical documents for a certain period. Isn't that why?

Oswald: The purple folder is an internal bank document. There is no legal requirement related to it. Once used, it can be discarded.

Adelaide: So, if we send digital payment files to Finance, we won't have to print the purple folder anymore?

Andrew: We won't need it.

Oswald: If the data is in an integrated workflow platform, you won't even need to send the files. The Finance Department can access the data online.

It was as though they had finally toppled the first in a huge array of dominoes, and the inevitable cascade was beginning. Adelaide was disconcerted. It was possible to simplify the process and eliminate a range of activities that generate cost but no value. She realized that she would have to justify past expenses and felt threatened.

Adelaide: We've invested heavily in a top-of-the-line printer to print the purple folder reports! What now? What are we going to do with it?

Oswald: Send it to Legal. We can put it to good use there.

Adelaide: What will happen to the people who work on the purple folders?

Me: There's no shortage of work at the bank. We now need to understand how to optimize the use of our resources to generate the best possible result.

I confess that I felt a little sorry for her. Imagine a person discovering that they had spent their entire life watering a plastic plant.

Andrew, on the other hand, was euphoric about the possibilities.

Andrew: Making data available in an integrated system will not only save money by eliminating unnecessary work but also help the bank earn money by optimizing cash flows. Integrating this process on a single platform will bring enormous returns to shareholders.

We designed the sequence of activities, eliminating those that don't add value and optimizing the sequence. With the entire process on a single workflow platform, the new supplier payment process was redesigned without breaking up departments and allowing finance to adjust cash flows even before expenses were accounted for.

Supplier Payment TO-BE Flow

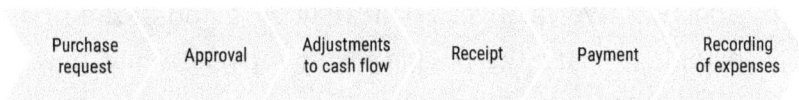

Purchase request	Approval	Adjustments to cash flow	Receipt	Payment	Recording of expenses

In addition to being much simpler, this process allowed the bank to invest its working capital with more liquidity and less risk.

Imagine how a short-sighted person feels when they put on a pair of glasses for the first time, and the world comes sharply into focus. Everyone was like that, taking stock of reality as if they had just woken up from a long and confusing dream.

> Adelaide: I have to say that I'm still a little shocked. When I started working in Accounting, the purple folders already existed, and I never questioned their importance. I didn't think having a big-picture view was that important.

I'm not sure that Adelaide's mindset completely changed from output-driven to outcome-driven that day, but it was certainly an important step for her to evaluate her way of thinking and acting.

A change of mindset doesn't happen in a single moment, like turning a key or pressing a button. It requires daily effort and dedication to act as desired. When you think about it, it's not just thinking that affects how you act. The opposite can also work for developing a mindset. We can influence our feelings and thoughts by deliberately acting as we believe appropriate.

In the end, I didn't do too badly in the role of business analyst. We finished the workshop by mapping out requirements for integrating the financial and accounting systems, which would bring several benefits to the bank. I felt as if I had won an Olympic medal. I was inspired to continue using business analysis practices to help more people think about the world holistically, with a focus on outcomes.

Chapter 27: Community

I left for the weekend with a feeling of "mission accomplished" and the commitment to meet with Oscar on Monday to define the next steps for the transformation of the corporate culture in the organization. The result of the workshop showed that it was possible to transform the mindset to be outcome-driven through the practice of business analysis. Using the techniques and discussing real situations, we were able to:

- transform the participants' way of thinking, awakening them to the effectiveness of solutions from a holistic view,

- influence their feelings so they were open to listening and felt confident enough to make the necessary transformations, and

- see their change in attitude, taking the lead to discuss and challenge current work models with creative proposals for innovation.

It was a great victory, but I still didn't know how to do it on a larger scale to spread the mindset collectively and transform the company's entire corporate culture.

Certainly, the people who participated in the workshop would become transforming agents in their areas and could positively "contaminate" other co-workers, but the opposite effect could also happen. Over time, they could lose enthusiasm and revert to the old output-driven mindset. We needed to create a support network for innovation projects and celebrate each breakthrough as a victory so that those involved would feel motivated to continue to be guided by outcomes.

All this would be the subject of my meeting with Oscar on Monday. Until then, I had a weekend full of activities and was looking forward to them.

On Friday night, I had a romantic dinner to celebrate Julia's enrollment in the therapeutic companion course. She was pleased and excited. In addition to fulfilling her love for caring for children, her new specialization would pay much better. Soon, she'd be earning more than she had earned as a lawyer.

On Saturday, there was lunch at Rodrigo's house. He had decided to cook some meals at home for friends on weekends, and everyone paid a fixed price, as in a common restaurant, to eat outstanding food. Beyond that, he had started taking orders for frozen dishes and already had a waiting list. It was only a matter of time before he left the Call Center and dedicated himself to gastronomy full-time. Everyone noticed this, and Rodrigo himself already seemed to have decided.

It's easy to understand my enthusiasm for Friday dinner and Saturday lunch, which promised to be delicious; however, to my surprise, I was also excited to participate in a professional event on Sunday. I never thought I'd feel excited to work on a weekend. I truly had been transformed! But to be honest, it wasn't exactly about work. Throughout the day, I would participate in a business analysis conference, at which Barbara was one of the speakers.

I had never been to an event like that and didn't know what to expect. I was curious to meet people with the same profile as Barbara, who transformed organizations by focusing on outcomes and using business analysis techniques as I had done during the last few days. I imagined most participants would be IT people, which scared me a little. Would I fit in? Or would I feel like a fish out of water?

The event took place in a convention center with approximately 300 participants. Upon arriving, I went to the accreditation counter, where a girl gave me a warm smile, a booklet with the event agenda, and a badge with my name and title: "Innovation Analyst — State Bank." I felt important.

There were several rooms where simultaneous lectures would be given, and I had to choose those I wanted to attend. A table with coffee and cookies was in a central space, and a few people were standing around talking. Around this table, companies sponsoring the event had booths selling preparatory courses for certification or modeling and information management software for business analysis. I didn't know a single soul. I wasn't sure what to do or where to put my hands. Awkward didn't even begin to describe it. Totally out of my comfort zone, I decided to approach the table and busy myself with a cup of coffee.

> Ricardo: Hello! Good morning. Nice to meet you. Welcome to our event. I see that you are an innovation analyst at the State Bank. What an interesting position! It's not very common. What does an innovation analyst do?

Ricardo arrived with a huge smile and started a conversation, treating me like an important guest. He was president of the local chapter of the International Institute of Business Analysis[7] and, as far as I could understand, one of the event organizers. He wanted to know about me and how we worked on innovation at the State Bank, but I had more questions than answers for him.

> Me: To be honest, I'm still figuring out what an innovation analyst does. It's a new position created to change mindsets and focus the corporate culture on outcomes rather than outputs.

> Ricardo: That's very interesting! Did you see on the agenda that we will have a lecture on strategy analysis using OKRs before lunch? I think it will interest you.

> Me: I haven't seen the agenda yet.

> Ricardo: Filip will be the presenter. There he is. Hey,

---

7. IIBA (International Institute of Business Analysis) is a non-profit association with volunteer-run regional offices in various parts of the world. These offices are called chapters.

Filip, come here! Tell us a little bit about what you're talking about today.

Filip: Hello! Nice to meet you. I'm presenting some strategies to ensure organizational changes persist and don't evaporate at the end of projects.

Me: That sounds fascinating!

In addition to the speaker and the president, other participants interested in innovation and change joined our conversation. Without any effort, I was already integrated and felt like part of the community.

It was a pleasant surprise to discover that many people were experiencing situations similar to mine with the same doubts and challenges. Although working in different organizations and positions, we feel a strong bond created by the focus on valuable outcomes and the holistic and collaborative way of thinking about business.

Most of the participants were indeed from IT, and most of the lectures were oriented toward work related to computerized systems projects using slightly more technical language. I imagine that, in large organizations, it's difficult to make any organizational transformation that doesn't involve changes in computerized systems. I thought that the projects defined in our innovation workshop would also involve changes in systems. "Business and IT aren't so distant," I thought.

During the event, I also met other professionals who weren't directly related to technology but sought to make organizational transformations from different perspectives:

business architects, product managers, process analysts, quality assurance analysts, risk analysts, consultants, business managers, and individual entrepreneurs. Many people saw value in learning and practicing the techniques and concepts of business analysis, and their experiences generated valuable ideas to be applied in each context.

Barbara's presentation took place after lunch. It was one of the most prestigious. The room was full, and only then did I realize I wasn't her only fan. Barbara is a well-known speaker in the field and many people were eagerly waiting for her tips on conducting meetings and dealing with stakeholders in difficult situations. I felt grateful that I had already received valuable tips from her before my workshop and could confirm her ideas most certainly worked. At the end of the presentation, a line of people formed to talk to her and take pictures. I stood at the end of the line and waited my turn.

Me: Wow, Barbara. You're a rock star!

Barbara: Not at all! People here are very kind and eager to learn more effective ways to transform the organizations where they work. You should present the work from the Innovation Department as a case study at the next conference.

Me: Me?! Present in front of everyone, just like you did? I don't know if I have the courage. I've never done this before.

Barbara: You had also never conducted a workshop before, and, as far as I know, you did an excellent job.

My cheeks flushed, and I smiled awkwardly. I was delighted to receive recognition for my work from an admired role model. True, I was already comfortable as a conference attendee, but imagining myself as a speaker was too much. What would I have to share with these people that might be helpful to them?

I thought about our workshop, the materials we created using business analysis techniques, the transformation of the participants' behaviors, and the feedback at the end. As I recalled all this, it seemed to me that it was no small feat.

> Me: What do you think of a presentation titled "The Outcome-Driven Mindset"?

> Barbara: I think it'll be a great success.

I thoroughly enjoyed participating in the conference. I made several friends and connected with people from different companies on social networks with a promise to keep in touch and exchange experiences in the future. I had arrived feeling alone and left feeling the exact opposite. "I found my tribe," I told Julia, as soon as I saw her that night. She couldn't even take it in properly. She was distressed and anxious to tell me something.

> Julia: Did you see the news?

> Me: What news?

> Julia: It was announced this afternoon. The State Bank has been sold.

Chapter 28: Start Over

The sale of the State Bank to an international financial group took everyone by surprise. From my first conversation with Oscar, I knew that the bank wasn't doing well and was struggling to keep up with the competition. However, I had believed there would be time to transform the organizational culture, recover the prestige of the past, and reinstate the bank as "the most innovative retail bank in the country," as described in its vision. Unfortunately, there wasn't.

On Monday morning, tormented by a griping stomachache, I arrived for work amid an atmosphere of insecurity that enveloped everything and everyone. People were stupefied and milled around uncertainly. Upon entering the beautiful building where the board of directors convened, I saw them replacing the State Bank sign with the name of the international financial group. I took the elevator to the floor where Oscar's office was, still beautiful with its wooden furniture and fresh flowers. I noticed that the beautiful receptionist wasn't at her desk. She was sitting on the little sofa in the reception area, scrolling on her cell phone.

Me: Good morning. I have a meeting scheduled with Oscar for this morning.

Receptionist: I'm sorry, but all meetings have been canceled.

Me: Isn't Oscar here?

Receptionist: No, and none of the directors either. The entire board has disappeared, and we've been told to cancel all appointments. We're waiting for more information.

Me: So what should I do?

Receptionist: I have no idea. I'm here preparing for what's ahead and looking for other job opportunities. If new directors come from abroad, I'm history. I can't even speak their language.

Me: Don't worry, everything will work out.

I said that out of compassion but without any conviction. I had no idea if everything would work out or even what "work out" meant in that situation. I was speaking as much to myself as to the receptionist. It was what I wanted to hear and believe, but it was hard. I didn't know what to do, and I couldn't think straight with the pain in my stomach. The activities that Oscar had delegated to me were concluded last Friday with the closing of the innovation workshop. My next steps were to be decided in that day's meeting with him. A meeting that might not take place now. There was no way to know what would happen to the Innovation Department in the new company.

I went to HR to talk about my situation and on the way, I met Mr. Andrade.

Me: Geez, that came out of the blue! Did you know that the bank was being sold?

Mr. Andrade: No. I don't think even the directors knew. Only the president and the executive board. With this change, all innovation projects are frozen until a new strategic direction is defined.

Me: It's a bit of a letdown! But our project is well-grounded and should be implemented, don't you think?

Mr. Andrade: I don't know. The group that bought the bank is huge and has branches worldwide. In a change like this, I think they'll implement their standard methodology and use the systems they use everywhere. I wouldn't be surprised if they decided to close our Call Center and outsource our entire operation.

Me: My God, that sounds ominous! Do you think all our efforts in the workshop will be lost?

Mr. Andrade: Not at all! Maybe the projects won't move forward, but they weren't the main outcome of the workshop. The main outcome, for me, was a change of mindset and a lesson for life. I can honestly tell you that the changes that lie ahead don't scare me. My feeling today is one of curiosity and even a little excitement. The bank needed radical change, and I don't know if the Innovation Department alone could have done it. Sorry for being so direct.

Me: Don't be! I also had concerns about our ability to transform the entire organization's corporate culture.

Mr. Andrade: Now we'll have to change everything, and everyone will be impacted. I'm excited to put what I've learned into practice in the Call Center or wherever I can help.

Mr. Andrade surprised me once again. With this courageous and flexible stance, he could adapt to whatever came his way.

In HR, I met with Clarice and shared my insecurities with the convivial matriarch who always gifted us with chocolates and a positive message to cheer us up.

Me: Clarice, I need your advice. I was going to define the new activities of my work today with Oscar, but he didn't come, and I don't know what to do.

Clarice: I'm going to confide in you some information that no one knows yet, but HR has already been told. More than half of the directors have been fired, and Oscar is among them. He doesn't work at the bank anymore.

The pain in my stomach stabbed harder, and an acidic taste came up the back of my throat.

Me: And when will we know who the new director of innovation will be?

Clarice: I must ask you to keep this confidential for now—the Innovation Department will be dissolved. The international group that acquired the bank doesn't have such a department in its structure and doesn't intend to deviate from the global standard, so Oscar was fired in the first wave.

In addition to my stomachache, I felt dizzy, and my legs were wobbly. Exactly when we were in a position to significantly impact the organization, with a defined project portfolio, committed sponsors, a validated mindset transformation model, and the energy to expand our outcome-driven approach, I saw everything topple like a house of cards.

> Me: What will happen to me? My current position is innovation analyst.

> Clarice: I believe that the position will be eliminated as well. I can't relocate you back to the Call Center because your current salary is incompatible with the agent role, and the company's policy prevents salary reduction. We'll have to wait and see where to fit it in with the guidelines we're given. But don't worry! We'll find something for you.

"Don't worry" is the phrase my body needed to hear but seemed to refuse to understand. At least, my stomach, head, and legs didn't seem to have understood. I felt like I was running a fever in response to an unknown virus.

> Me: Thank you, Clarice. I'm glad to know that I can count on your support. But until the new guidelines arrive, what should I do?

> Clarice: Keep doing your job until further notice.

> Me: But what is my job?

She looked around, leaned closer, and spoke in a low voice:

> Clarice: For now, pretend you're busy and don't attract too much attention. Here! Take a chocolate bar with you. We'll talk in a few days.

I left HR feeling much worse than when I entered. My frustration was boundless.

Suddenly, I would have to hide in the shadows, pretending to be working. I felt demoralized, and my stomach hurt too much to eat that chocolate.

In the past, with an output-driven mindset, perhaps this would have been my dream job—getting paid to do nothing, my only task was to clock in when I arrived and left. But now, with an outcome-driven mindset, it was a punishment! Something that made no sense at all. I want to work with a purpose!

I went to the clinic to see if they would give me something to make me feel better. A competent, experienced nurse examined me. I didn't have a fever, but my blood pressure was significantly higher than normal. He told me to take the rest of the day off.

> Nurse: Have a rest and come back tomorrow! Several people have been through here today with symptoms like yours.

> Me: Is it a virus?

> Nurse: If I didn't know what was happening today, I might think it was a virus. But in the current context, I'd

say it's a panic attack. You need to chill out. Don't worry! We'll still be here tomorrow, and the day after tomorrow, and the day after that.

That exact phrase again: "Don't worry." I felt like a total fraud! I argued that we needed to be brave and motivated to face challenges, and there I was, paralyzed by anxiety, scared to death, and full of uncertainty. But that wasn't the only way to face the situation.

Looking at it from a more holistic point of view and open to different perspectives, maybe this was the best way to transform the State Bank. The president and board may have made a sound decision to sell the bank before it completely collapsed. A radical change, with a whole new culture implanted from a foreign vision, could promote economic growth and prosperity in our community. Why not? It was better than going bankrupt due to the inability to compete with fintech companies. I needed to compose myself and keep my focus on the expected outcomes. I needed to be creative and discover opportunities to improve results. No matter where I worked, I could adapt.

As I left the bank, I registered my exit on the time clock and swiped my card at the turnstile to access the lobby and go out into the street. I stopped momentarily and thought: Here was an opportunity for improvement! Time-card controls are easy to falsify. I could leave my card with a colleague to swipe later, and no one would even know I had left early. An integrated system between HR and Security could authorize my entry and register my presence at work in a single action. If this system used biometric reading, such as fingerprint reading or face recognition, it would no longer be possible for one person to impersonate another. An interesting innovation!

On the way to the subway, I stopped at a pharmacy to buy something for my stomachache. The clerk asked me the name of the medicine I wanted to take, and I said I didn't know. I wanted him to recommend something based on my symptoms, but he couldn't. Only the expert pharmacist could do this, and he wasn't available. I asked for a generic antacid, and while I was paying, I thought about how a remote service business could be structured with pharmacists on duty to serve people in all the pharmacies in the country. A self-service pressure gauge and an automated auscultation system would be connected to a service computer with a camera and microphone. Thinking about these possibilities for innovation made me feel a little better.

At the subway station, I had to buy tickets. The self-service machines were almost all broken, and there was a huge line at the human service counters. I decided to wait at the machines and watched people select the number of trips and insert a credit or debit card to issue the tickets that would be inserted into the subway turnstile. I kept thinking that the subway ticket is a type of currency that you can exchange exclusively for transportation. When I buy a ticket, I exchange money, which can buy a range of things, for another type of money exclusive to transportation. Why do I need to make this switch? Why can't I swipe my credit or debit card directly at the subway turnstile and pay for my transportation directly? It was an obvious system integration that must certainly have been implemented elsewhere in the world.

Thinking about these opportunities for improvement everywhere, and how my mindset helped me identify them easily, made me feel much better. I didn't even take the antacid in my pocket. My stomachache had disappeared. Walking through the subway station toward the point where I would catch my train, I already felt refreshed. I remembered that it was this way, leaving work early one day, that I had met Julia on the subway platform and talked to her for the first time.

I was lost in my thoughts as my train approached the station, and I heard a sound I hadn't heard for a long time in the distance. Someone hitting the strings of a very out-of-tune toy guitar and singing in a very high-pitched voice:

> *Let life take me; life takes me!*
> *Let life take me; life takes me!*
> *Let life take me; life takes me!*
> *I am happy and grateful for all that God gave me!*

It was the old lady with the toy guitar. It could only be her! Julia and I had already looked for her downtown and at several subway stations to no avail. At that moment, I couldn't see her, but I could hear her voice somewhere in the station, and I tried to identify which direction it was coming from.

> *Let life take me...*

Gradually, the train approached, and its noise grew louder and louder, drowning out the music to the point where I could no longer hear it. I looked everywhere, but there was no sign of the old woman. As soon as the train stopped, people left the cars. It was noisy, preventing me from hearing the music.

I decided not to take the train and wait for the next one. I was curious to see where this story would take me.

With the train leaving the station and people on their way out, silence reigned again without any sign of the old lady or her toy guitar. Could I have imagined the song? Was it my unconscious sending me a message? Something related to gratitude and availability for whatever lay ahead? I had no idea, but I would have to wait at least 10 minutes until the next train. I had decided to sit on a bench when my phone started ringing.

> Oscar: I'm glad I caught you! I apologize for not attending our appointment earlier today, but I have good news.

Oscar told me that his day had been hectic. Over the weekend, he had learned he would be dismissed from the State Bank and immediately contacted executives from other companies. He hadn't spent a single day unemployed and was hired at once by a giant service company to transform its corporate culture by making it more innovative.

> Oscar: I told them what we did at the State Bank, and they can't wait to implement the outcome-driven mindset in all their departments. They loved the simplicity of the framework and were enthusiastic about the approach to transforming people through business analysis. Please come to work with me as innovation manager. Our objective is to set up a Center of Excellence in business analysis, bringing together

people from all areas to share good practices, create innovation opportunities, and develop skills. What do you say?

And that was how the doors opened for me onto a new train—one that would take my journey to a much larger scale than the workshops of the previous week. In this new job, I'd be responsible for creating an outcome-driven corporate culture transformation in all the departments of one of the largest companies in the country.

Me: Of course I will. You can count on me!

From the depths of the subway tunnel, a light pierced the shadows, and the rumble of the approaching train gradually filled the space. Yet, through the din, I heard it again—the faint but unmistakable strum of a toy guitar. This time, it wasn't just a whisper of curiosity pulling me back. It felt like something closer to clarity, illuminating a new but uncertain path forward.

The familiar sound echoed through my mind. I thought of Julia, my constant rhythm amid the complexity of life. I thought about the future I wanted to build, not for myself, but with her.

Tonight, I'd take the next step.

Epilogue

This is a fictional story, but I hope you can relate to it. The characters and reports described here were inspired by situations I've experienced in almost three decades of work as a consultant and instructor specializing in business analysis in companies from various sectors, including finance, insurance, public, third sector, energy generation and transmission, basic sanitation, and software development.

Some of the exchanges in this book are from real conversations adapted to the company context of this narrative.

I hope you feel encouraged to study and become an agent of change, as the protagonist did.

Only two characters in this story are real: Dona Rosa and the old lady who plays the toy guitar and asks for money.

Dona Rosa passed away in 2015. Her son is still my neighbor, and his family maintains the tradition of celebrating Three Kings Day every January 6th.

During the period in which I provided services for B3, the São Paulo Stock Exchange, I came across the old lady playing "Let Life Take Me" with her children's guitar practically every day on the sidewalk of downtown São Paulo near Praça da Sé. Since the day I gave her the money from Dona Rosa's charm, I have never seen her again. If anyone knows her whereabouts, please let me know. I hope she's well.

Fabrício Laguna

Appendix: Outcome-Driven Mindset

The way an individual thinks shapes their actions.

Some individuals perform only their tasks without question.

The outcome-driven mindset is a way of thinking based on a holistic view, which generates analytical and collaborative behavior.

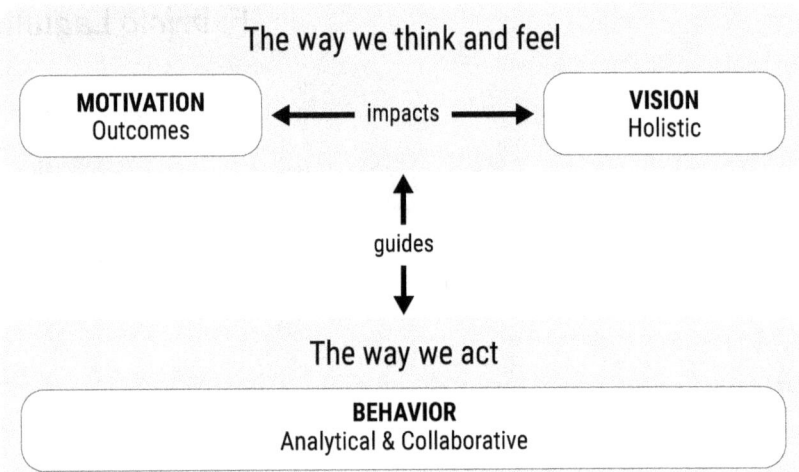

The way we think and feel

MOTIVATION		VISION
Outcomes	← impacts →	Holistic

↑
guides
↓

The way we act

BEHAVIOR
Analytical & Collaborative

Mindset is the predisposition of individuals to think, feel, and act the way they usually think, feel, and act. When this pattern is repeated within an organization, we call this collective mindset the corporate culture.

To achieve better outcomes, an organization must intentionally transform its corporate culture, starting with how all employees think.

Summary Table

	Output-Driven Mindset	Outcome-Driven Mindset
THINK	**Limited** I worry about my own success.	**Holistic** I understand value for everyone.
	Compliant I am responsible for doing things right.	**Effective** I am responsible for making sure the right things get done.
FEEL	**Averse to Debate** I have no patience for differing opinions.	**Open to Listening** I am sensitive to different personalities and their unique needs.
	Fearful I feel uncomfortable when there is ambiguity or uncertainty.	**Bold** I love learning new things. Challenges motivate me.
ACT	**Rigid** I resist change and avoid new ideas.	**Adaptable** I always challenge the status quo.
	Obedient I follow explicit instructions without question.	**Creative** I figure out how to achieve the best result.
	Individualistic I ignore other points of view.	**Collaborative** I take responsibility for collaboration and shared understanding.

About the Author

Fabrício Laguna is one of the leading voices in business analysis in Brazil—and beyond. With over 25 years of experience as a consultant, instructor, and speaker, he has helped major organizations in finance, insurance, and government modernize their practices, bringing agility, clarity, and a sharp focus on business value.

As Senior Advisor to the president and CEO of IIBA (International Institute of Business Analysis), Fabrício contributes to the development of world-class business analysis content. He is also the founder and partner at Gigante Consultoria, a firm specializing in training and consulting in business analysis, project management, and systems thinking.

Holding CBAP, CPOA, PMP, and AAC certifications, Fabrício is an author, content creator, and educator whose videos, articles, and online courses have reached students in over 70 countries. Known for his ability to make complex concepts easy to understand, he brings humor and clarity to his teachings, whether in the classroom, on stage, or online. Fabrício is a former president of the IIBA Brazil Chapter and a frequent speaker at international conferences and contributor to publications.

Learn more about his work at TheBrazilianBA.com or connect with him on LinkedIn.com/in/fabriciolaguna.

Acknowledgements

A special thanks to Renata Cortez for reviewing the original Portuguese version of this book, Gina Gato for translating it into English, and Robert McClements for the final review. Gratitude to IIBA for their encouragement and support in publishing it. And a big hug to the global business analysis community, which has become like family to me.

www.ingramcontent.com/pod-product-compliance
Lightning Source LLC
Chambersburg PA
CBHW071157210326
41597CB00016B/1583